I0012904

Inside the Silicon

How Microchips Are Designed and Made

By

Ethan Maxwell

Ethan Maxwell

Copyright 2024 Ethan Maxwell. All
Rights reserved. No part of this publication
may be reproduced without the consent of the
author.

"What a computer is to me is the most remarkable tool that we have ever come up with. It's the equivalent of a bicycle for our minds."

--Steve Jobs

Ethan Maxwell

Table of Contents

Ethan Maxwell

Introduction

In the palm of your hand lies a marvel of human ingenuity – a device that connects you to the world, captures memories, and performs countless tasks. At its heart beats a tiny powerhouse: the microchip. These minuscule marvels are the unsung heroes of our digital age, silently orchestrating the symphony of modern life.

From the moment you wake up to your smartphone alarm to the instant your car's safety systems protect you on the road, microchips are working tirelessly behind the scenes. They are the brains of our smart homes, the engines of scientific discovery, and the catalysts of innovation across industries. Yet, for many, the intricate world of microchips remains a mystery.

"Inside the Silicon: How Microchips Are Designed and Made" invites you on a fascinating journey into the heart of this technology. We'll peel back the layers of these complex creations, revealing the artistry and precision that go into their design and manufacture. You'll discover how a grain of sand transforms into a powerhouse of computation, and how teams of brilliant minds collaborate to push the boundaries of what's possible.

Ethan Maxwell

Chapter 1: The Building Blocks of Technology

What is a Microchip?

Microchips are often seen as the quiet champions of today's tech world. They work behind the scenes, making sure our devices function smoothly, much like how a bustling city's control center manages traffic lights and street signs to keep everything moving safely. It's tough to picture our lives without these tiny wonders, as they are now an integral part of our everyday experiences.

At their essence, microchips are small semiconductor devices packed with various electronic parts like transistors, diodes, and capacitors. They handle countless tasks, ranging from simple math to complex data processing, making them vital to almost every electronic device we rely on. Whether you're using a smartphone, a laptop, or a smart thermostat, microchips are the smart brains that make it all happen.

When we think of "microchip," we might picture a shiny metallic piece of technology. However, it's important to remember that microchips aren't just one thing; they're carefully designed and built from various materials through complex processes. Their main job is to process and store information, which lets our devices perform tasks we often take for granted. They do this incredibly fast, completing millions, or even billions, of instructions every second.

To truly understand the importance of microchips, it helps to look at their history. The adventure of the microchip started in the late 1950s when computers were massive machines that filled entire rooms and needed a lot of resources just to do simple tasks. Everything changed with Jack Kilby's invention of the first integrated circuit in 1958, followed by Robert Noyce's silicon-based chip. These groundbreaking innovations made it possible to shrink computer size while boosting their capabilities.

As technology moved forward, microchips became more powerful. The 1970s marked the beginning of the microprocessor, a type of microchip capable of handling a wide range of tasks. This opened the door for early personal computers and set the stage for a surge in affordable consumer electronics, the rise of the internet, and the digital revolution that changed our lives in countless ways.

In the decades that followed, advances in design and manufacturing kept pushing microchip technology forward. The number of transistors on chips skyrocketed, with modern processors now cramming billions of transistors into a space no bigger than a fingernail. This rapid miniaturization, often referred to as Moore's Law, suggests that the number of transistors on a microchip doubles about every two years, resulting in incredible growth in processing power. Today, microchips can tackle complex tasks that once required supercomputers.

Microchips aren't just found in computers and smartphones; they're essential parts of a wide range of devices that shape our lives today. In cars, microchips manage everything from how the engine runs to vital safety features. In medical devices, they keep track of important health metrics and provide targeted treatments. In our home appliances, they enable smart features and energy-saving options. Their presence in so many areas shows just how crucial microchips are; they truly form the backbone of modern technology.

Moreover, microchips do more than just power devices; they also spark innovation. With the growth of artificial intelligence, the Internet of Things (IoT), and advanced robotics, the need for more powerful and efficient microchips has skyrocketed. As we keep pushing the limits of what technology can do, microchips will be at the center of this transformation, enabling breakthroughs we can hardly imagine today.

In short, microchips are key players that drive the functionality of countless devices across various fields. They have developed from simple integrated circuits into sophisticated processors capable of performing complex calculations and managing intricate systems. The influence of microchips is immense, shaping how we engage with technology and guiding the future of innovation. As we dive deeper into this exciting topic, it becomes clear that understanding microchips is fundamental to appreciating the very heart of modern technology and the countless ways it enriches our lives.

From Atoms to Silicon

Silicon may seem like an ordinary element, but it plays a crucial role in the story of technology. This simple metalloid, which we find in abundance in the earth's crust, is the backbone of modern microchip technology. To picture where silicon comes from, think about the grains of sand on a warm beach, the clay along riverbanks, and the quartz rocks that dot the landscape. With an atomic number of fourteen, silicon is more than just a number; it's a vital resource that has changed our lives in countless ways, many of which we don't even notice.

The journey of silicon from its natural state to the highly engineered materials used in microchips is a captivating tale filled with mining, refining, and transformation. Silicon is sourced from some of the most mineral-rich areas on our planet. Countries like China, the United States, and Brazil are among the largest producers, where you can find vast amounts of silicon dioxide—often called silica—hidden in sand, quartz, and other minerals. This natural wealth makes silicon a readily available resource, and it's the first step in turning it into a key player in technology.

Mining for silicon is like going on a treasure hunt. Workers use massive machines to dig deep into the earth, sifting through tons of rock and sand to find this precious element. It's a demanding process, requiring a lot of manpower and investment in equipment. Once the raw silica is collected, it undergoes several refining steps to get rid of impurities and make it pure enough for semiconductor use.

The refining starts with crushing the silica ore, which is then heated in a furnace, sometimes reaching temperatures as high as 1,500 degrees Celsius. This extreme heat causes a chemical change, breaking down the silica into silicon. The result is a material known as metallurgical-grade silicon, which is about 98-99% silicon—still not pure enough for making microchips.

To reach the level of purity needed for electronics, additional refining is necessary. One common method is chemical vapor deposition (CVD). In this process, silicon reacts with a halide precursor, like silicon tetrachloride, at high temperatures. The silicon is then deposited onto a substrate, resulting in a layer of ultra-pure silicon. This step shows one of silicon's most remarkable traits: its ability to undergo chemical reactions that yield materials with very different properties.

Silicon's unique chemical characteristics are key to its role in microchips. At its core, silicon has four electrons in its outer shell, which lets it create strong bonds with other elements, especially when mixed with dopants like phosphorus or boron. This ability to create semiconductors is similar to how a sponge soaks up and releases water. When silicon is doped, it can either gain extra electrons (n-type) or create holes where electrons are missing (p-type), allowing it to conduct electricity under the right conditions.

Think of silicon as a playground, where adding certain elements opens up new games to play. Just a small amount of dopants can completely change how silicon behaves, turning it into a great conductor and allowing it to act as a switch—an essential function in microchip technology. This flexibility is what makes it possible for transistors to fit onto silicon wafers, which are the building blocks of microchips.

The transformation from raw silicon to polished silicon wafers is a blend of art and science. These wafers, often buffed to a shiny finish, serve as the stage for intricate microchip designs. The journey from unrefined ore to a finished wafer involves several steps, including slicing, polishing, and cleaning, each step vital to ensuring that the final product meets the strict standards of the semiconductor industry.

As we look into the various stages of silicon refinement, it's inspiring to see the technological advancements that have made these processes more efficient and eco-friendly. Over the years, innovation has played a huge role in reducing waste and cutting down the carbon footprint linked to silicon production. Techniques like closed-loop water systems and energy-efficient furnaces have emerged to promote sustainability in mining and refining. This move towards being environmentally responsible reflects a larger trend in the tech industry toward smarter production and consumption practices.

However, while silicon is the reigning champion of microchips, the world of semiconductor technology is constantly changing. Researchers are now investigating alternative materials that could work alongside or even replace silicon in certain applications. Notable options include gallium arsenide, which offers better electron mobility, and graphene, a single layer of carbon that has astonishing electrical and thermal properties. The search for these materials isn't just about improving performance; it's also a response to the growing demands of a world that relies more and more on efficient computing.

When we think about the future of silicon technology, it's important to stay open to what lies ahead. Although silicon has served us well for many years, the needs of new technologies—like artificial intelligence, quantum computing, and advanced telecommunications—may eventually lead us to explore new materials that can support the next wave of innovation. Looking into these alternatives doesn't mean we're turning our backs on silicon; it acknowledges that we may need a variety of solutions to tackle the complexities of our technological landscape.

Reflecting on the journey from atoms to silicon, we see a story filled with transformation, innovation, and adaptability. From its humble beginnings in nature to its complex role in powering the devices that define our lives, silicon represents more than just a material; it symbolizes human creativity and our unyielding drive for progress. Its development mirrors the path of technology itself—a journey marked by both challenges and victories—and invites us to wonder what the future may bring. The realm of microchips is indeed fascinating, but it's just one chapter in the larger story of silicon's importance in our lives.

Everyday Microchips

It's truly amazing to realize just how deeply microchips have woven themselves into our everyday lives. Most of us don't even notice they're there, quietly working behind the scenes. Whether we're enjoying a hot cup of coffee in the morning or using the high-tech navigation system in our cars, these tiny chips are the brains behind it all. Microchips have become the silent heroes of our modern world, and taking a moment to understand their importance helps us appreciate the complexity of our surroundings.

Let's kick things off with a common household appliance that we often take for granted: the microwave. Picture your breakfast routine—heating up leftovers, defrosting that forgotten piece of chicken, or warming up your coffee. Hidden inside this everyday appliance is a microchip that manages power levels, tracks cooking time, and ensures our food is cooked just right without burning it. In seconds, this small chip processes information and sends commands, all while we focus on our morning tasks. It may go unnoticed, but the microchip is like a conductor, orchestrating the perfect blend of heat and timing in our kitchens.

Next, think about the refrigerator, the steadfast companion of every kitchen. It's not just a box for keeping food cold; it's a smart machine filled with microchips that help control the temperature, keep track of door openings, and even alert us when we accidentally leave the door ajar. These chips work hard to keep our groceries fresh, helping us reduce waste and save money. Many modern fridges come with smart technology that allows us to check what's inside from our phones and even suggests recipes based on what we have. Thanks to microchips, our kitchens have become more convenient and environmentally friendly.

Personal gadgets are another area where microchips shine. Our smartphones, those handy little computers we carry everywhere, are prime examples of how widespread microchip technology has become. Each phone contains several chips that handle everything from processing data and running apps to managing calls and connecting to the internet. Just think about it! Microchips let us send texts, snap high-quality photos, play games, and even keep track of our heart rates, all from the palm of our hand. Without microchips, the smartphone boom would have remained just a dream, lacking the speed and efficiency that we now consider normal.

Tablets, too, rely heavily on these tiny processors to deliver entertainment and educational content. The smooth experience of flipping through photos, watching movies, or chatting with friends over video calls is made possible by the delicate networks of microchips working together. These gadgets have changed how we consume information and connect with others, turning our world into a tight-knit community where we can reach out to anyone, anywhere, at any time.

Now, let's shift our focus to the realm of cars. Today's vehicles are packed with technology, and microchips are at the heart of it all. They help manage everything from optimizing engine performance to cutting down emissions, as well as running infotainment systems that offer navigation, music, and connectivity. Imagine driving a car that uses GPS to find the fastest route while considering live traffic updates. That's a microchip working hard to analyze loads of information in real-time, making our driving safer and more enjoyable.

Microchips also play a big part in the growing world of smart home technology. Devices like smart thermostats that learn our heating preferences or security cameras that alert us to motion are all powered by microchips. For instance, a smart thermostat like the Nest not only lets us control home temperatures from afar but also adapts to our habits over time, saving energy and reducing costs. It's a fantastic blend of convenience and efficiency, showing how microchips can transform our living spaces into smarter environments.

We can find real-life examples of microchip innovation in the stories of families that have embraced smart home technology. Take a busy family with kids and pets, for example. To manage their heating, cooling, and security needs, they installed a selection of smart devices. Thanks to the microchips in these gadgets, everything works together seamlessly, allowing them to adjust the temperature from work and receive alerts about any unusual activity while they're out. This not only gives them peace of mind but also helps lower their energy bills, highlighting the real benefits that microchips can bring.

As we explore the landscape shaped by microchips, we can't ignore the new trends that are changing our daily lives. The Internet of Things (IoT) has emerged, connecting everyday items to the internet and to each other through microchips. Picture smart refrigerators that can automatically reorder groceries or fitness trackers that keep tabs on our health. The IoT is creating a network of connected devices that enhance our lives in countless ways. Imagine a home where the lights dim when you start a movie, your coffee maker kicks in when your alarm goes off, and your thermostat adjusts to your preferences before you even get home—all thanks to microchips communicating effortlessly with each other.

Wearable technology is another exciting area driven by microchips. Fitness trackers and smartwatches keep an eye on our health metrics in real-time, giving us insights about our activity levels, heart rates, and sleep patterns. Being able to see this information at a glance helps us stay aware of our health and encourages us to make better lifestyle choices. In essence, the microchip acts like a personal health coach, gathering and analyzing data that can lead to healthier habits and improved well-being.

Microchips are also making waves in healthcare. In the world of personalized medicine, they are at the forefront of innovations that could change how we manage our health. From advanced diagnostic tools that analyze patient data and recommend tailored treatments to implants that monitor vital signs, microchips are reshaping how we understand and approach healthcare. They're enabling earlier detection of medical issues, ultimately resulting in better outcomes for patients.

As we think about the influence of microchips, it's fascinating to imagine what the future holds for this technology. Smart cities, where everything from traffic lights to public transport is interconnected and responsive, are on the horizon. Imagine a city that optimizes traffic flow in real-time, easing congestion and improving transportation—all thanks to systems driven by microchips. We're already seeing the testing of autonomous vehicles, which rely on microchips to navigate, communicate, and keep passengers safe.

Moreover, as microchips continue to evolve, the integration of artificial intelligence opens up even more exciting possibilities. Picture a car that not only drives itself but also learns your preferences, adjusting its route based on your favorite stops or even suggesting new paths based on current events or weather. We might even see personalized health monitoring systems that can predict health issues before they escalate, allowing for timely interventions.

The excitement around these advancements is contagious, and as we step into this new era, it's important to recognize how microchips will shape our daily lives. The potential for this technology to drive progress and innovation is limitless. With each breakthrough, we move closer to a future where technology seamlessly blends into our routines, enriching our lives and enhancing our well-being.

In the grand story of human progress, microchips are the quiet architects of our modern world, weaving their way through our homes, our cars, and even our bodies. The leap from simple transistors to the complex systems we have today is truly remarkable. Each microchip reflects the dreams and creativity of countless innovators working to make the world a better place. As we look ahead, we can only be amazed by the possibilities on the horizon.

Microchips have not only changed our present but have also set the stage for a future that is more efficient, interconnected, and responsive to our needs. As we navigate this exciting new landscape, let's stay curious and open to the innovations that microchip technology is sure to bring. The future is not just a fantasy; it's a reality waiting to be explored, powered by the incredible potential of microchips that keep reshaping our everyday lives.

Ethan Maxwell

.

Chapter 2: The Blueprint of Innovation

Conceptualizing a Chip

In a world where technology is a part of our everyday lives—from the smartphone you carry to the smart fridge that keeps track of your groceries—the microchip is like a hidden hero. It's the powerful engine that makes all these modern devices work. But how do we even start to think about what a microchip is? Where did these tiny, yet mighty components come from? The journey of a microchip—starting as an idea and becoming a working product—is an exciting adventure filled with creativity, scientific exploration, and engineering skill.

At the core of creating a microchip lies a crucial idea: understanding what people need. Before any design gets underway, it's vital to recognize the wants and needs of consumers and industries. Engineers and innovators carefully look at the tech landscape, searching for gaps, challenges, and opportunities. They tune in to emerging trends and pay attention to feedback from existing products. This process often feels like a dance, where intuition meets real-world data, leading to fresh and inventive ideas. While some might picture inventors as lonely figures working away in labs, the truth is often much different. It's usually a collaborative effort, involving teams that include not only engineers, but also marketers, designers, and trend watchers.

Picture a brainstorming session at a tech company where a lively group of people gathers around a table covered in coffee cups and leftover pizza. Ideas fly around like a pinball bouncing in a machine, with each suggestion building on the last. It's in this energetic atmosphere that the seeds of a new microchip are planted. One person might propose a chip that saves energy, while another imagines one that boosts connectivity. These conversations aren't just empty chatter; they are key moments that help shape the future of technology.

Once an idea starts to take shape, it's time for the innovators to get to work and turn that concept into reality. This is when the plans for the microchip begin to come together. The process is a bit like urban planning, where city planners have to think about the layout of streets, buildings, and parks. In chip design, engineers must carefully plan how to arrange transistors, capacitors, and circuit pathways. Each part has its own job, and how they're arranged can significantly affect how the chip performs. Engineers use special software known as Electronic Design Automation (EDA) tools to create detailed designs and layouts. These tools help visualize the chip's architecture, setting the stage for the complex flow of electricity that will one day buzz through it.

As the design moves forward, engineers enter the stage of prototyping and simulation, much like an architect building a model before starting a new construction project. During this crucial phase, simulations become invaluable. Using advanced algorithms and computer models, engineers test how the chip will operate under different conditions. They examine everything from heat distribution to electrical interference, often going through several design revisions before settling on a final version. This step requires patience and attention to detail, as even a tiny flaw can lead to major problems once the chip is made.

This thorough testing phase is not just about striving for perfection; it's about ensuring reliability. Much like a chef who tastes and tweaks a recipe before serving it, engineers need to guarantee that their microchip will work smoothly when it hits the market. The virtual environment of simulations allows them to adjust settings, enhance performance, and refine the design until it meets the high standards expected in today's tech world.

As we explore the details of creating a microchip, it's clear that this process involves many different fields. The mix of creativity, technical skills, and market insight drives innovation. The engineers, designers, and marketers each contribute their unique perspectives and expertise, creating a chip that is not just advanced but also meets user needs and market demands.

While the path from idea to reality can be long and complicated, it's the blend of imagination and precision that leads to groundbreaking technology. A microchip may be small in the grand scheme, but its influence is far-reaching, affecting everything from the latest smartphone features to how efficiently industrial machinery operates.

In this exciting world of ideas and inventions, the process of imagining a microchip highlights the endless possibilities ahead. As technology continues to move forward at lightning speed, the future of microchip design is set to venture into new territories. From artificial intelligence to quantum computing, the chips we develop today will lay the foundation for advancements we can only start to envision.

Through this look at conceptualizing a chip, we gain an appreciation for not just the detailed designs and engineering talents that go into these devices, but also the human creativity and teamwork that make it all happen. This intricate dance of innovation will push us onward, shaping our world in ways that connect, empower, and enhance our lives. Each microchip tells its own story, showcasing human ingenuity and offering a glimpse into the exciting technological wonders that lie ahead.

Designing the Architecture

When we think about microchips, it's easy to get caught up in the final product—the sleek, powerful devices that power our modern world. But to really appreciate the magic of microchips, we need to understand the detailed architecture that makes these tiny wonders tick. Microchips are made up of different core components, each playing an important role in how the chip works. Transistors, resistors, capacitors—they might sound like something from an electronics textbook, but each piece contributes something special to the overall design of the microchip.

Transistors are often called the building blocks of electronics. You can think of them as tiny switches that turn on and off at lightning speed, allowing electricity to flow through the chip. In many ways, they are like the brain cells of the microchip, processing information as they pick up signals. A single microchip can hold billions of these transistors, all working together to perform complex calculations. The scale of this arrangement is mind-boggling, much like a busy city where everyone has a specific job but together creates the dynamic life of the city.

To help you picture this, think about a light switch in your home. When the switch is off, no electricity gets to the bulb, and the room is dark. But when you flip the switch on, electricity rushes through the wires, lighting up the space. Just like that, a transistor can be either "off" (no current flowing) or "on" (current flowing), enabling the circuit to do its job. Thanks to the ability of transistors to switch states so quickly, microchips can process data at astonishing speeds, allowing us to browse the internet or play video games without a hitch.

Now let's talk about resistors, which are components that limit the flow of electrical current. If transistors are brain cells, you can think of resistors like traffic lights at busy intersections, making sure that the electrical flow stays in check. By regulating the current, resistors help protect delicate components from harm and keep everything running smoothly. Imagine trying to drive through a city without traffic signals—chaos would likely follow! Resistors play a similar role, guiding electrons along their paths while keeping order in the circuit.

Capacitors also play a key role; they act like little storage units for electrical energy. Think of them as water tanks in a plumbing system—holding water and releasing it when needed. In a microchip, capacitors temporarily hold electrical charge and let it go to help keep voltage levels steady. This is really important for maintaining smooth performance, especially when power demands change quickly. Without capacitors, the microchip would struggle to keep everything running right, leading to unpredictable behavior.

As these components—transistors, resistors, and capacitors—come together, they create a network known as circuits. You can liken these circuits to highways where electrical signals travel, with each component acting as a stop along the way. The arrangement of these components and how they interact shapes the overall architecture of the microchip, affecting its performance and capabilities.

Now that we've covered the basic parts of microchips, let's turn our attention to the design methods that engineers use to build these complex structures. Different strategies, like top-down and bottom-up designs, offer unique ways to tackle the challenges of microchip architecture.

In a top-down design approach, engineers start by looking at the big picture of the entire system before diving into the specifics. Imagine planning a city: you'd first consider the overall layout—the positions of parks, major roads, and neighborhoods—before getting into the details of individual buildings and streets. This broad view helps designers see how each part fits into the larger context, ensuring that every piece serves a purpose that aligns with the chip's intended functions.

On the flip side, the bottom-up design method begins with the individual components, building the architecture piece by piece. Here, engineers carefully create each transistor, resistor, and capacitor before putting them together to form larger circuits. You can think of it like constructing a complex model with Lego blocks, where each piece must fit perfectly to create a sturdy structure. This method is especially useful when working with new components or when the properties of individual parts are crucial to the overall design.

As engineers decide between top-down and bottom-up approaches, they also consider different architectural models, especially RISC (Reduced Instruction Set Computing) and CISC (Complex Instruction Set Computing). These two models represent different philosophies in chip design, each with its benefits and drawbacks.

RISC architectures focus on keeping things simple and efficient, using a limited set of straightforward instructions that can be executed quickly. You can think of RISC as a sleek sports car—designed for speed and agility, it zips around the track without the extra weight of unnecessary features. This streamlined approach allows RISC chips to achieve high performance while consuming less power, making them perfect for devices like smartphones and tablets where battery life matters.

On the other hand, CISC architectures pack in a broader range of complex instructions into one chip. Think of CISC like a luxury SUV, loaded with features, plenty of cargo space, and the ability to handle a variety of terrains. While it's more powerful and versatile, that complexity often leads to higher power usage and slower performance compared to RISC. CISC chips are typically preferred in systems that need intensive computing power, like personal computers and servers, where the trade-off between power and performance makes sense.

When engineers choose an architectural model, they need to consider how it will affect performance, power consumption, and the specific applications it's suited for. A well-rounded microchip design has to strike a careful balance among these factors to meet the needs of its intended use. For example, a chip designed for a battery-operated device must focus on power efficiency to extend battery life, while a chip made for high-performance computing may prioritize maximum speed and processing power.

In our digital age, where performance and efficiency are crucial, the choices made during the design stage can have wide-ranging effects. Just like an architect designing a skyscraper must think about how it looks, its structural integrity, and its impact on the environment, microchip designers must navigate the challenges of today's and tomorrow's tech demands. Decisions made during the design phase can shape not just the chip's capabilities but also the future direction of technology in various fields.

As we think about the careful design process behind microchips, it's clear that this field blends creativity with engineering skill. Designers must not only have technical knowledge but also nurture a spirit of innovation, always pushing the limits of what's possible. The architecture of microchips becomes a canvas for this creativity, where every choice shapes the final product, much like a sculptor carving a block of stone until a masterpiece emerges.

The journey from raw materials to a finely-tuned microchip showcases human ingenuity at its best. It involves many considerations, from choosing components to deciding on the overall design philosophy, all aiming to create devices that improve our lives. The interconnectedness of transistors, resistors, capacitors, and the thoughtful methods used to build them highlight the complexity of microchip architecture.

Through our exploration of microchip design, we gain a solid understanding of how these amazing devices are built. The intricate dance between creativity and engineering not only leads to powerful chips but also drives the ongoing evolution of technology. As we stand on the edge of new breakthroughs—like artificial intelligence and quantum computing— the architecture of microchips will keep changing, reshaping our world in ways we're just starting to imagine.

So, the next time you look at your smartphone or marvel at what your laptop can do, take a moment to appreciate the artistry behind the design of microchips. Each device is a harmonious blend of electrical engineering, where transistors, resistors, and capacitors each play their part in perfect unison. The microchip is more than just a collection of components; it represents the brilliance of human creativity and teamwork, driving our society toward an exciting, tech-filled future.

Simulating Performance

In the exciting world of microchip design, simulation is the quiet hero, working behind the scenes to make sure that the detailed blueprints created by engineers turn into real, functioning silicon wonders. Picture trying to navigate a maze without a map. That's what it would be like to tackle the complexities of microchip functionality without simulation. Not only does simulation guide the way, but it also serves as a testing ground where engineers can play out different scenarios and choices before rushing into physical production.

At its heart, simulation allows engineers to predict how a microchip will act in the real world. Long before a single transistor is etched onto silicon, engineers use cutting-edge software to create virtual models of their designs. These models help them visualize how the chip will function under various conditions, spot potential problems, and fine-tune performance—all without the costs and time that would come with making physical prototypes. The magic of simulation is that it uncovers flaws and inconsistencies that might not be visible during the initial design stage.

One of the most crucial types of simulation in chip design is functional verification. This stage is vital because it confirms that the microchip operates as it should. Engineers run thousands of test cases, mimicking different inputs and conditions to see how the chip reacts. It's a lot like a dress rehearsal for a play—actors go through their lines and movements to catch any hiccups before opening night. By throwing a range of scenarios at the chip—some expected and others completely off the wall—engineers can identify performance issues early on, saving both time and resources later.

Timing analysis is another key simulation method that engineers rely on. When designing a microchip, timing is everything. Just a tiny delay of a few nanoseconds could lead to significant performance issues or even total failure. During this phase, engineers examine how signals travel through various parts of the chip. They measure how long it takes for signals to move and ensure everything stays in sync. Think of it as tuning a finely crafted orchestra— if one musician is slightly out of sync, the whole performance can sound off. Timing analysis helps engineers make sure that every component works together seamlessly.

Another important aspect of simulation is power estimation. As technology continues to evolve, the need for energy-efficient designs becomes increasingly urgent. Engineers must predict how much power their microchip will use under different operating conditions. To do this, simulation tools model the power consumption of various design configurations, guiding engineers in making smart choices about which components to include and how to structure the design for the best energy efficiency. It's similar to trying to forecast your monthly electricity bill before the month starts; that's the kind of foresight power estimation provides.

Even with all the advancements in simulation technology, the journey has its challenges. Engineers often face unexpected interactions between components or unforeseen performance problems that can complicate things. One engineer shared a story about how a newly added component caused a ripple effect of issues. "It was like introducing a new player to a well-rehearsed sports team," he explained. "Suddenly, all the plays we practiced didn't work anymore. We had to take a step back and reevaluate everything."

This back-and-forth nature of chip design is where simulation truly shines. Engineers don't see simulation as a one-off task; they treat it as an essential part of their process. Each round of design and simulation builds on the last, allowing for ongoing improvements and adjustments. While this repetition can be tedious, it's a necessary part of creating solid designs that can handle real-world demands.

To give you a clearer sense of how simulation plays out in practice, let's walk through a typical scenario engineers might face. Imagine a team tasked with designing a new microcontroller for wearable fitness devices. They start by building a virtual model of their chip, including all the necessary components—transistors, resistors, capacitors, and some cleverly designed interfaces.

Once the initial design is ready, the engineers dive into a series of simulations. They kick off with functional verification, inputting various data packets to see how the chip responds. Perhaps they simulate a user doing different exercises, sending heart rate and activity data to the chip. During this phase, the team carefully reviews the outputs, making adjustments and tweaking the design whenever discrepancies pop up. There's a real buzz in the room—each successful simulation gets them closer to a working product.

Next, the engineers focus on timing analysis. They painstakingly measure how long it takes for the chip to process incoming data, checking the signal paths to make sure everything functions within acceptable limits. If they find that a particular signal is taking longer than expected, they'll need to rethink their design—maybe by changing the layout or adding a new component to boost performance. This balancing act requires both technical skill and creative problem-solving.

Finally, the engineers turn to power estimation. They run simulations to forecast the chip's power use during various activities, like tracking heart rate while the user is resting or during tough workouts. The goal is to ensure that the chip can work efficiently without draining the battery too quickly. The engineers are thrilled with the results, realizing that a well-optimized design enhances the user experience and prolongs the device's battery life.

As they conclude their simulations, the team reflects on their journey. Each twist and turn has provided them with new insights, leading to a more polished design. They recognize the crucial role simulation has played—not just in pinpointing flaws but also in encouraging teamwork and innovation. "It's like being in a band," one engineer remarked. "Each simulation teaches us something new, and we learn to play off one another's strengths."

The significance of simulation in microchip design is hard to overstate. It bridges the gap between theory and real-world application, allowing engineers to test their ideas in a safe and controlled setting. The continuous cycle of simulation fosters exploration and experimentation, enabling designers to push the limits of what's possible.

In an industry where precision and performance matter most, simulation has become an essential tool. It not only helps engineers catch flaws early on but also empowers them to innovate and optimize designs for a fast-changing technological landscape. As microchips continue to shrink and grow more complex, the importance of simulation will only increase.

The path from the initial idea to the final product is filled with countless iterations and adjustments—all made possible through the power of simulation. It's a testament to the ingenuity and commitment of engineers who, with the right tools and a drive to innovate, work to create microchips that will shape the future of technology. Whether it's a microcontroller in a basic fitness tracker or a processor driving an advanced artificial intelligence system, the ability to simulate performance ensures that these devices will live up to their promises.

As we stand on the brink of exciting new technological advances, it's vital to grasp the importance of simulation in microchip design. It reinforces the idea that successful engineering isn't just about creating something that works; it's about making something that works incredibly well. The intricate dance of design, simulation, and refinement shapes the devices that are part of our daily lives, blending creativity with engineering precision to pave the way for the future.

Simulation is more than just a tool; it's a key part of the creative process, helping engineers envision what lies ahead. This blending of technology and artistry transforms the microchip from just a collection of components into a smart, high-performance solution that meets the demands of our increasingly complex world. So, the next time you enjoy the features of your favorite gadgets, remember the invisible but vital role that simulation played in turning those innovations into reality.

Chapter 3: Translating Ideas into Schematics

From Concept to Schematic

Turning an idea into a detailed microchip design can feel like taking a simple melody and transforming it into a complex piece of music. Every note, pause, and rhythm needs to work together to create a symphony that is both functional and meaningful. In the realm of microchip design, this transformation is a team effort that combines technical skills with creativity, communication, and a good dose of innovation.

At the start of this journey, the idea is often just a spark—an abstract thought born from a need or a problem that needs solving. Picture a group of engineers huddled around a whiteboard, each mind buzzing with possibilities. One person proposes a chip to boost processing power in mobile devices, while another brings up energy efficiency. Yet another imagines how it could be used in artificial intelligence. In this lively exchange of ideas, the groundwork for what will eventually become a detailed schematic is laid.

Collaboration is key in this process. Engineers, designers, and other stakeholders come together, each offering their own insights and expertise. This mix of perspectives creates an environment rich in creativity and innovation, allowing initial concepts to grow and be refined. Everyone challenges each other's ideas, contributing to a cycle of exploration and experimentation where new possibilities can thrive.

Once the core ideas are set, it's time to turn those thoughts into a visual format. This is where the fun of schematic design begins. Engineers use specialized software to create diagrams that show how the microchip will work. These visuals are crucial because they serve as a common language, helping all involved—engineers, designers, project managers, and even marketing teams— understand complex ideas quickly.

Imagine the schematic taking shape like a blueprint for a stunning building. Every line and symbol has meaning; each one represents a key component needed for the chip's operation. This stage requires careful attention to detail. Engineers meticulously draft logic gates, connections, and circuitry that will dictate how the chip behaves. It's a painstaking process, as even a tiny mistake can lead to major problems later on. Balancing creativity with technical accuracy is vital; without it, the design risks falling short.

Additionally, the role of software tools is incredibly valuable. Today's designers have access to advanced applications that make the design process smoother and more efficient. These tools not only help in drawing schematics but also allow engineers to run simulations, testing their designs' functionality before production begins. This ability reduces the chance of errors and inefficiencies, ultimately saving both time and resources.

As the designs come together, communication and teamwork remain crucial. Feedback loops are a fundamental part of this journey. Team members share drafts of the schematic, exchanging critiques and suggestions openly. This back-and-forth process ensures that the final product is a well-rounded reflection of the original idea, enriched by the different insights gathered along the way. It's this collaborative spirit that enhances the design, creating a schematic that not only represents the chip but also captures its intended functionality.

The journey from concept to schematic is also marked by a constant drive for efficiency. Designers and engineers keep a close eye on optimizing space, power use, and performance. Microchips often face limits like size, heat production, and energy consumption. This is where creativity meets analytical thinking. Engineers need to think outside the box, finding new ways to pack more functionality into smaller spaces without hampering performance.

Take, for instance, a microprocessor designed for a smartphone. The team starts with a concept for multi-core processing. As they dive into the schematic design, they realize they must balance performance with thermal management to prevent the chip from overheating during heavy tasks. This insight leads them to focus on optimizing the design to incorporate efficient cooling solutions, such as innovative layouts and heat sinks.

As the schematic develops, it becomes more than just a functional guide; it also serves as a communication tool. It captures the essence of the design and reflects the collaborative effort of the team. For stakeholders, this schematic provides clear insight into how the microchip operates and what it aims to accomplish. A well-crafted schematic could mean the difference between a project that thrives and one that struggles.

The shift from concept to schematic is a dynamic blend of creativity, teamwork, and technical know-how. It's a process that calls for patience and adaptability, as ideas evolve through discussions and revisions. The end product is a detailed schematic that lays the groundwork for the chip's development, turning abstract thoughts into a tangible reality full of potential for innovation.

In our fast-changing technological landscape, understanding this transformation from concept to schematic is more important than ever. The capability to visualize ideas and turn them into designs leads to the creation of microchips that power everything from smartphones to advanced artificial intelligence systems. The artistry of microchip design lies not just in technical skills, but in the imaginative thinking that drives these designs forward, ensuring they are both functional and groundbreaking.

So, as we dive into the world of microchip design, it's clear that the journey from abstract ideas to detailed schematics is an exciting expedition, fueled by collaboration, creativity, and a relentless quest for efficiency. This process ultimately shapes the technology woven into our daily lives, influencing the future in ways we are just starting to grasp.

Logic Design

The world of microchip design is filled with fascinating ideas, built on a foundation called logic design, where abstract concepts meet real electrical signals. At the core of this intricate system is Boolean logic, a mathematical framework that underpins digital circuits. To grasp how microchips function, it's important to start with the basic building blocks that make them work: binary values and logic gates.

Binary values, which are simply 0s and 1s, represent the most basic form of data in computing. Think of a light switch: when it's off, it's a 0, and when it's on, it's a 1. This binary system allows us to communicate with microchips, converting complex ideas into a language they can understand. The beauty of using this system lies in its simplicity. Just as one light switch can control a light, binary values can manage a whole range of operations within the microchip. Each electrical signal, whether it's a high voltage (1) or low voltage (0), translates into a decision that drives the chip's performance.

To get a clearer picture of logic design, we need to familiarize ourselves with logic gates, the basic components of digital circuits. Think of these gates as the gatekeepers that determine how inputs work together to produce outputs. The simplest types of these gates are the AND, OR, and NOT gates.

An AND gate is like a two-way street where traffic can only flow when both directions are clear. In digital terms, this means that both inputs must be true (or "on") for the output to be true. Imagine having to show both a keycard and a password to enter a secure building. If either is missing or incorrect, access is denied. This analogy captures how an AND gate operates: it requires all conditions to be satisfied to produce a positive result.

Then there's the OR gate, which works in a completely different way. This gate is like a party invitation—if at least one person shows up, the party is on! In logical terms, if at least one input is true, the output will also be true. Imagine you want to go out for dinner. If either your friend or your partner can join you, you're set for a night out. This inclusive approach of the OR gate highlights its flexibility in digital logic.

Next, we have the NOT gate, a unique member of the logic gate family. This gate flips the input. So if the input is true (1), the output will be false (0), and vice versa. Picture a light switch with a twist: when the switch is on, the room is dark, and when it's off, the room is bright. The NOT gate is essential in more complicated logic circuits, helping engineers manipulate and control the flow of information effectively.

By combining these basic gates, we can create more advanced circuits that perform a wide range of tasks. When engineers put together AND, OR, and NOT gates in different ways, they can build arithmetic circuits that can add and subtract. For instance, consider a half-adder circuit, which takes two binary digits and adds them together, producing a sum and a carry output. It's impressive how the interaction of these gates results in such complexity from fairly simple principles.

Beyond just arithmetic, these logical operations help microchips store information and make decisions. Picture a microchip going through a complicated decision-making process: it receives various inputs, assesses them through its logic gates, and then comes to a conclusion. This might be whether a device should turn on or off or how much data to process based on incoming signals. The ability of microchips to make decisions comes directly from the clever integration of logic gates, which act like the brain behind the actions.

As we look back at the development of logic design, we can't forget the pioneers who laid the groundwork for modern digital logic. George Boole, a mathematician and philosopher from the 19th century, introduced what we now call Boolean algebra. His work created a way to handle logical statements, which opened the door for future advancements in computing. Fast forward to the 20th century, and we meet Claude Shannon, a key figure often called the father of information theory. Shannon took Boolean logic and applied it to electrical circuits, providing a theoretical base for digital circuit design. His groundbreaking work empowered engineers to design complex systems that could intelligently process information.

These historical moments in logic design are more than just facts; they represent the evolution of ideas that turned abstract concepts into practical tools that drive our modern world. The microchips we depend on today are the result of years of research, development, and the real-world application of these foundational ideas. Each gate and circuit design represents a piece of a larger puzzle that engineers have been working to solve over time.

The deeper we dive into logic design, the more we appreciate how these principles come together to create functioning microchips. Manipulating binary values with logic gates is not just a technical skill—it's a kind of art. It enables the creation of systems that can learn, adapt, and respond to many inputs, ultimately powering the technology that shapes our everyday lives.

Think about the impact of this logic design in your daily devices. Every smartphone, computer, and appliance is built on the same principles we've talked about. When you send a text message or scroll through social media, your device is performing billions of logical operations every second. The smooth operation we often take for granted is the result of careful logic design, where abstract ideas become real-world applications.

The field of microchip design is a captivating mix of ideas and principles. From the basic binary values to the intricate logic gates that make computation possible, understanding logic design helps us appreciate the technology that surrounds us. It allows us to see beyond the surface, recognizing the complex structures and historical contributions that make our digital age a reality.

As we keep exploring microchip design, let's remember that this journey is not just about understanding how chips work but also about appreciating the creativity and innovation that drive progress. Logic design is a testament to human ingenuity, showing us that with the right ideas, we can turn abstract thoughts into real-world realities that impact our lives. So, the next time you flip a switch, send a message, or interact with any digital device, take a moment to think about the intricate logic at work, quietly creating the seamless technology we've come to rely on.

Designing for Efficiency

In the world of microchip design, where every little detail counts, the drive for efficiency feels like both an art and a science. As technology evolves at lightning speed, the need for microchips that are not just powerful but also energy-efficient becomes even more urgent. Today, a microchip is more than just a simple collection of transistors and circuits; it's a carefully arranged collection of parts designed to perform at their best while using as little energy as possible. Think of it like a high-performance athlete: just as athletes need to manage their energy and body heat during tough workouts, microchips also need to monitor their power and temperature for optimal performance.

One of the smartest ways to achieve energy efficiency in microchips is through a technique called power gating. Picture a smart home where you can turn off appliances remotely when they're not in use—that's the basic idea behind power gating. By selectively shutting down parts of a microchip that aren't active, engineers can dramatically reduce energy use. It's like a well-organized kitchen where you only turn on the stove when you're ready to cook, avoiding the waste that comes from running everything at once.

The beauty of power gating is in its simplicity and effectiveness. Let's take a microprocessor with multiple cores, each capable of tackling different tasks. When one core isn't busy—say it's waiting for input or handling a light workload—it can be turned off or switched to a low-power mode. This doesn't just save energy; it also keeps heat levels down, similar to how an athlete might cool off between intense training sessions to prevent overheating.

But what happens when certain parts of a microchip are powered down? That's where heat management becomes crucial, another key factor in achieving efficiency in microchip design. Heat can be a big problem; too much of it can cause a chip to throttle, meaning it slows down to avoid overheating. Therefore, engineers need to create systems that work efficiently while also managing heat effectively.

Imagine an athlete running a marathon; they need to maintain an ideal body temperature to perform at their best. They might hydrate, wear breathable fabrics, or use cooling techniques to keep their body heat in check. Similarly, microchips must be designed with thermal considerations at the forefront. Techniques for thermal management include using heat sinks, thermal pads, and even advanced materials that disperse heat more efficiently. By thoughtfully arranging components, designers can create easy pathways for heat to escape, preventing buildup that could slow performance.

Moving from power management to the physical layout of a microchip, it's crucial to highlight how the design of circuits can maximize space efficiency. In this competitive industry, smaller often means better; compact designs lead to quicker communication between parts, which translates to improved device performance.

Think about a busy city; the way streets are laid out can greatly affect traffic flow. When streets are organized with shorter distances and fewer traffic lights, cars can move smoothly and quickly. The same goes for microchip design; by reducing wire lengths and optimizing where components are placed, engineers can cut down on latency. When parts are closer together, the electrical signals don't have to travel as far, leading to faster response times.

The arrangement of components on a microchip isn't just about looks; it's a carefully thought-out strategy that directly affects how well it performs. Engineers have to consider various factors when designing the layout, such as how signals will time out, the chance of interference, and the overall flow of electricity. Each component needs to be positioned so it can communicate smoothly with its neighbors, much like a well-choreographed dance where each movement is planned and purposeful.

Beyond traditional 2D layouts, engineers are also looking upwards, diving into 3D stacking of circuits as an exciting new area in microchip design. Imagine this method like organizing books in a library—not just stacking them on flat shelves but creatively using vertical space. By stacking layers of circuits on top of each other, designers can save valuable space while improving heat management.

This approach allows for shorter connections, less power usage, and better performance. It's like building a multi-story parking garage instead of spreading out a single-level lot. Not only does 3D stacking make the most of available space, but it also opens new doors for integrating different components closely together, leading to performance boosts that traditional layouts simply can't offer.

Using new materials and technologies is also key to evolving microchip design towards greater efficiency. For example, engineers are increasingly looking at advanced materials like graphene and carbon nanotubes, which have amazing electrical and thermal properties. These materials can help reduce energy loss and boost performance, paving the way for next-generation microchips that use only a fraction of the power compared to their predecessors.

However, designing for efficiency isn't just about better performance; it's also about being responsible to our planet. Sustainability and environmental impact are hot topics in today's tech world. As microchips become more energy-efficient, they help lower overall energy consumption across devices, contributing to the global effort to fight climate change. The results can be astounding; when millions of devices operate efficiently with less power, the total energy savings can be significant.

Plus, as both manufacturers and consumers start to prioritize eco-friendly technology, demand for sustainable microchip design will only grow. Engineers have a chance to lead the way in creating solutions that align with a more thoughtful society. By focusing on efficiency in their designs, they can ensure that the tech innovations we enjoy today don't come at the cost of future generations.

As we navigate through this complex world of microchip design, it's clear that striving for efficiency is not just a technical hurdle but a significant duty to society. Engineers, equipped with smart strategies and the latest technologies, face the important task of creating a future where our devices are not just powerful but also sustainable. Each step taken towards energy-efficient microchip design brings us closer to a greener, more sustainable world.

The delicate balance of power management, circuit layout optimization, and material innovation reveals a realm of possibilities. Microchips, the unsung heroes of our digital era, are in the midst of a transformation that challenges us to rethink what efficiency means in technology. As engineers continue to explore new methods and materials, the next generation of microchips promises to be more than just functional; they will represent a commitment to sustainability and a vision for a brighter future.

Ultimately, the journey of microchip design is one filled with creativity, innovation, and responsibility. Just like an athlete prepares for peak performance while being mindful of their health, engineers must also design microchips that improve our lives while caring for the planet. This blend of efficiency and sustainability isn't just a trend; it's a critical shift that will shape the next chapter of technology, ensuring that as we move forward, we also respect the world we live in. Each microchip created marks a step towards a more efficient, responsible, and sustainable technological landscape, and it's an exciting journey that is just beginning to unfold.

Chapter 4: The Art of Circuit Design

Circuit Layout Fundamentals

In the ever-evolving world of technology, microchips quietly power all the smart devices we can't live without—from the sleek smartphone in your pocket to the smart thermostat that learns your heating preferences. But behind the curtain of these amazing gadgets lies a complex web of circuits, meticulously organized to perform countless tasks. To truly grasp how this works, we need to look at the basics of circuit layout, which is the heart of microchip design.

Think of circuit design like drawing the blueprint for a skyscraper. Just as an architect carefully plans where each wall and window will go, considering both style and structural safety, engineers must thoughtfully arrange the elements of a microchip. The first step in this exciting journey is to identify the key components that will make up the circuit—resistors, capacitors, and the star of the show, transistors.

Resistors act as the traffic controllers for electric current, regulating flow and ensuring that voltage levels stay balanced throughout the circuit. You could think of them as the stoplights at a busy intersection, guiding the current smoothly and preventing potential traffic jams that could lead to circuit failures. Then we have capacitors, which are like little energy tanks. They temporarily hold electric charge, similar to how a water tower stores water, ready to release it when there's a sudden increase in demand.

The real heroes in circuit design, however, are the transistors. These tiny switches control whether the circuit is on or off, making decisions that enable the processing and storage of information. It's astonishing to see how far we've come—what used to fill a room now fits in the palm of your hand, with billions of transistors crammed into a single microchip. Because of this, how we arrange these components can greatly affect performance, power use, and heat generation.

This is where schematic capture comes into play. Think of it as the first step in turning ideas into actual designs. During this phase, engineers create detailed drawings that show how the components connect to each other. By visualizing how resistors, capacitors, and transistors relate, engineers can better understand how the circuit will work. This step is crucial for spotting potential problems—like short circuits or voltage drops—before they become real issues in the final design.

Just like architects have to follow building codes and zoning rules, circuit designers face their own set of challenges. One major concern is managing heat. As circuits run, they produce heat, which can hurt both performance and lifespan. Engineers need to think about the thermal properties of materials and come up with strategies to cool things down, similar to how an architect designs ventilation systems to keep a building comfortable.

After the schematic capture, the next phase is layout design, where engineers determine where each component will sit on the microchip. This is like figuring out where to put the walls, windows, and elevators in a skyscraper. Engineers must think carefully about not only how components are logically organized but also how close they are to one another. The placement of each piece can influence signal clarity and unwanted electromagnetic interference.

Interference is a big deal, especially in tightly packed circuits. Every component generates some electromagnetic radiation, and when they're close together, the risk of noise affecting sensitive signals rises. Engineers have to use various tactics to reduce these effects, like shielding or carefully placing components to avoid interference. Plus, as the demand for faster speeds grows, having an efficient layout becomes even more crucial.

Additionally, space on a microchip is limited, making component arrangement a strategic challenge. Modern engineers often think outside the box, using algorithmic tools to optimize the layout while following strict design rules. These rules cover everything from how far apart components need to be to how layers can be stacked, all to ensure that the design can be produced effectively and reliably.

While circuit design may seem complicated, it's built on guiding principles that help engineers navigate the process. The way components interact, their layout, and the obstacles they face all play a part in creating microchips that are not only functional but also incredibly efficient.

Understanding the fundamentals of circuit layout opens a window into the world of modern technology. It highlights the creativity involved in design and the science that fuels progress. Every resistor, capacitor, and transistor is like a brushstroke in the masterpiece of microchip design. Each choice influences how the chip works, ultimately shaping the devices that define our daily lives.

As we dig deeper into circuit design, we start to see that this field is about more than just putting components together; it's about crafting experiences. The layout of a circuit impacts how devices perform, affecting everything from battery life to processing speed. In a world where efficiency and speed matter more than ever, the thoughtful design of circuits can really make a difference.

Next, we'll look at how these key principles are put into practice in real-world situations, showcasing how innovative engineers are constantly pushing the limits of what microchip technology can achieve. With every breakthrough, technology continues to evolve, giving us exciting glimpses into the future of microchips and their place in our rapidly changing world.

So, the microchip, which often goes unappreciated, stands as a testament to our engineering prowess and creativity. Each circuit designed brings us closer to a more connected, efficient, and intelligent future. As we move forward to explore the next fascinating aspect of this field, the design principles we've covered will remain crucial, guiding and inspiring the next wave of engineers and innovators.

Analog vs. Digital Circuits

The world of electronics is like a vibrant playground, filled with many different circuits that each have their own special job. Although they all aim to manage electrical signals that help us in our everyday lives, they do so in unique ways. At the core of this electronic landscape lies a key distinction: analog and digital circuits. These two types of circuits not only function differently but also come from differing philosophies about how to represent and manipulate signals. To picture this, think of a gentle stream flowing down a hillside—this embodies the nature of analog signals, which are smooth and continuous. Now, imagine a staircase where each step is clearly defined—this represents digital signals, which operate in distinct, binary steps.

Analog circuits work with signals that can change smoothly and continuously. Just like how a stream can shift its flow and direction without any sudden stops, analog signals can represent an endless range of values. This smoothness makes analog circuits particularly suited for applications where small differences matter, such as in audio and video. For instance, consider the warm sound of a vinyl record or the seamless transitions in a film. These rich experiences come to life thanks to analog circuits, which capture the delicate details of sound and light waves and transform them into electrical signals.

On the other hand, digital circuits thrive on the idea of discrete values. Much like a staircase with its well-defined heights, digital signals exist in specific states, often represented as a series of ones and zeros. This binary system enables digital circuits to handle information with incredible accuracy and reliability. Devices like computers and smartphones—tools we depend on daily—are built on this digital foundation. They utilize the clear-cut nature of digital signals to carry out complex calculations and manage vast amounts of data.

Now that we've explored the basic differences between these two circuit types, let's dig a little deeper into what makes them special and where we find them in action. Analog circuits, with their flowing signals, have a long-standing presence in audio gear. When you enjoy your favorite tunes on a classic record player, the analog system captures the subtle vibrations of sound waves. Every tiny change in pressure is transformed into an electrical signal that closely mirrors the original sound. Many music lovers believe that this results in a listening experience that feels richer and more genuine than what digital sound can offer. The warmth of analog sound has a unique charm that resonates with both musicians and fans, evoking a sense of nostalgia that digital sound often misses.

In contrast, digital circuits form the backbone of our modern computing world. They excel at processing binary information, converting zeros and ones into calculations, storing data, and running complex algorithms. Think about your smartphone: it's a marvel of digital circuits working together to run apps, manage connections, and provide instant information at the push of a button. The precision of digital signals means that every task is handled with high accuracy, which is crucial in situations where even the smallest mistake can lead to significant problems.

Real-world examples really help to shine a light on the differences between analog and digital circuits. Take an analog sound system, for example. When a musician strums a guitar, the strings vibrate and create sound waves that travel through the air. An analog circuit picks up these vibrations and converts them into an electrical signal that can be amplified and played through speakers, producing a rich sound that fills the space. The beauty of analog lies in its ability to capture subtle changes, making it perfect for audio applications where warmth and fidelity are key.

Now, think about the digital circuit in a modern computer. At its heart, the central processing unit (CPU) relies on digital circuits to perform calculations and make decisions. Each task that the CPU executes is divided into a series of binary steps, enabling lightning-fast processing speeds. Whether it's rendering graphics for a video game or running intricate simulations, digital circuits are designed to manage a wide range of tasks efficiently. Their accuracy and speed allow our devices to keep up with the demands of the digital age.

But the story doesn't stop here. As technology progresses, the lines between analog and digital circuits are starting to blend, giving rise to mixed-signal circuits that incorporate both elements. These circuits are vital in applications where the strengths of both types can be combined. For example, a digital camera uses mixed-signal circuits to capture images. The analog components process continuous light waves into electrical signals, while the digital parts convert those signals into the binary data that forms the final picture. This teamwork highlights the creativity and complexity of today's microchip designs, where the best of both analog and digital technologies come together to create groundbreaking solutions.

As we take a closer look at how analog and digital circuits interact, it becomes clear that each type has its advantages and drawbacks, and often the best choice depends on what you need to achieve. Analog circuits, with their continuous signals, shine in situations where detail and subtlety matter. They breathe life into audio and video experiences, capturing the essence of sound and light in ways that digital circuits can't fully mimic. Meanwhile, digital circuits are the champions of precision and speed, powering the devices that have changed our lives for the better. They excel in environments where accuracy is crucial and can effortlessly handle large amounts of information.

In an increasingly digital world, understanding the differences between these two circuit types holds great value. Each time you listen to a record, send a text message, or browse the internet, you're interacting with the unique principles of analog and digital circuits. Recognizing their roles helps us appreciate the technology we often overlook.

As circuit design continues to evolve, it pushes boundaries, blending analog and digital techniques to create more sophisticated and efficient systems. The innovations happening today are paving the way for the next generation of technology, where the relationship between analog and digital circuits will become even more complex. Looking ahead, the flexibility and creativity of these circuits promise to open new doors, changing how we engage with our digital world.

Understanding the differences between analog and digital circuits isn't just a technical detail; it's a key to appreciating how these technologies shape our lives. Each circuit we come across has a purpose, showcasing the skill and artistry behind our modern reality. Whether you find yourself swaying to the tune of an analog melody or being amazed by the speed of a digital process, embracing the variety in circuits deepens our appreciation for the technology that drives us forward.

As we move through the intriguing world of microchip design, the relationship between analog and digital circuits will remain a critical factor in the development of our technological landscape. With exciting innovations on the horizon, the story of these circuits is far from over. Each leap in design not only boosts performance but also opens the door for new applications, ensuring that both analog and digital technologies will continue to coexist and evolve together, shaping our future in ways we can only start to imagine.

Ensuring Reliability

In the fast-changing world of microchip technology, where millions of tiny transistors live on a single chip, reliability is incredibly important. The risks are significant, and the fallout from a failure can be disastrous. Picture a brand-new smartphone crashing right in the middle of an important video call or a medical device that inaccurately reads a patient's vital signs because of a faulty circuit. These situations not only ruin the user's experience but can also lead to serious consequences. The reliability of microchips isn't just a technical detail; it's a vital quality that can build or break a product's reputation and, in some cases, even put lives at risk.

Take the example of a major car manufacturer that had to recall a large number of vehicles due to a problematic microchip in their braking system. This chip, designed to ensure safety, failed under certain conditions, causing unexpected braking issues. The recall not only cost the company millions in expenses and hurt their brand image, but it also created fear among customers who depend on those cars for their safety. Incidents like this highlight why reliability in designing and making microchips is something we can't overlook. It's about trust, performance, and ultimately, human safety.

At the core of reliable microchip design is a deep understanding of the conditions these chips will face in the real world. Environmental factors such as temperature changes, humidity, and electrical noise can greatly affect a microchip's performance. This means engineers need to think ahead about the possible challenges their designs will encounter. This kind of forward-thinking is essential throughout the entire circuit design process and lays the groundwork for the careful testing and validation that follows.

To ensure that chips are reliable, engineers use a range of testing techniques during the design process. First, they run simulations to model how the microchip will perform under different conditions. Simulation software lets designers create virtual versions of their circuits, so they can investigate potential weaknesses without needing to build physical prototypes. This approach is highly efficient because it helps identify design flaws early on, before a lot of resources are spent on actual production.

Next comes prototype testing, where real chips are made and put through real-world conditions. This stage often includes stress tests that push the chips to their limits, checking how they handle extreme temperatures, voltages, and other tough conditions. For instance, a microchip designed for space travel must endure both the extreme cold of outer space and the intense heat generated during reentry into Earth's atmosphere. The information gained from these tests is invaluable for refining the design and making sure the chip will work reliably across the range of conditions it will face.

Automated testing equipment has also changed how we assess microchip reliability. In environments with high production rates, automation enables quick and consistent testing of many chips at once. Engineers can carry out numerous tests—evaluating signal quality, power usage, and various failure scenarios—ensuring that only the most dependable chips reach the market. The accuracy of automated testing also helps minimize human error, which further boosts the reliability of the final product.

Despite all these precautions, mistakes can still happen. That's where error detection methods come in. For example, parity checks offer a simple way to spot errors. By adding an extra bit to a group of data bits, systems can check if the information has been changed during transmission. If the parity check fails, the system recognizes that something went wrong and can take corrective action or send alerts.

Redundancy is another key strategy used to improve reliability. In situations where failure isn't an option—like in airplane systems or medical devices—engineers often include backup components. For example, a microchip that controls vital functions in an aircraft might have several backup systems ready to take over if one fails. This redundancy helps ensure that everything keeps running smoothly.

These strategies act like safety nets, catching problems before they escalate into serious failures. By working hard to implement thorough testing and error detection, microchip designers aim to produce products that aren't just functional but also trustworthy.

Even with meticulous testing and error-checking systems in place, some failures are unavoidable. This reality has led to the adoption of fault-tolerant design principles, which ensure that microchips continue to work even when some parts fail. This approach mirrors how systems in nature evolve to handle disruptions.

Redundancy plays a vital role in fault-tolerant design. Engineers might duplicate essential components so that if one fails, another can jump in and keep things running. For example, in a spacecraft, multiple processors might manage navigation and control. If one processor runs into trouble, the others can take over, ensuring the spacecraft stays on its planned path. This design philosophy not only boosts reliability but also gives users confidence in the technology they rely on.

Error correction codes (ECC) further enhance fault tolerance by allowing systems to spot and fix errors in data. For example, in computer memory, ECC helps detect single-bit errors and can automatically correct them, lowering the chances that a small mistake leads to big data loss or system crashes. This proactive way of handling errors strengthens microchips, helping them work well even when facing unexpected challenges.

Self-checking mechanisms are another clever feature of fault-tolerant design. These systems continuously monitor the health of different components, looking for signs of trouble before they affect performance. If a microchip notices something unusual—like a part overheating—it can automatically adjust how it operates or notify the user, allowing for prompt action. This self-awareness is like having a built-in guardian, keeping an eye on the system and ensuring everything runs smoothly.

The sophisticated process of creating reliable microchips showcases the creativity and skill of engineers in this field. By using a mix of testing techniques, error detection methods, and fault-tolerant designs, they develop microchips that can handle the challenges of real-life applications. The aim isn't just to meet standards but to exceed them, delivering products that people can trust in critical situations.

Looking ahead, the need for reliability in microchip design will only become more crucial. As devices grow increasingly interconnected and dependent on technology, making sure these systems work perfectly is more important than ever. The stakes are high, and engineers must keep pushing the boundaries and refining their reliability strategies, exploring new materials, technologies, and approaches.

In a world where microchips are the backbone of everything from our smartphones to life-saving medical devices, the quest for reliability remains a key driver of technological progress. Each innovation not only boosts performance but also deepens our understanding of how to create systems that can stand strong amid an ever-changing landscape. The commitment to ensuring reliability reflects a dedication to excellence, reminding us that each microchip carries the promise of a world that functions smoothly, efficiently, and safely.

Ethan Maxwell

Chapter 5: From Design to Mask

The Role of Photolithography

When you hear the term "photolithography," you might picture beams of light, optical lenses, and maybe a touch of magic. This process uses the incredible movement of photons to create the tiny building blocks of our modern world—the microchips that power our smartphones, computers, and countless gadgets that we rely on every day. At its heart, photolithography is a type of printing, but instead of ink on paper, it transfers detailed patterns onto silicon wafers with an accuracy that feels almost otherworldly.

The adventure starts with a design, usually crafted in advanced software where engineers carefully sketch out the blueprints for a chip. These designs are like intricate works of art—full of detail and requiring a level of skill that might be hard for some to see. What happens next is truly amazing: these designs are turned into a physical form through the photolithography process, acting as a link between the imaginative world of computer-aided design (CAD) and the real-world microchips.

To really grasp the importance of photolithography, you first have to recognize how crucial light is to the whole process. Photolithography uses ultraviolet (UV) light to project microscopic patterns from a photomask onto a light-sensitive layer called photoresist, which coats the silicon wafer. Imagine it like projecting a movie onto a screen, where the light selectively exposes certain sections of the photoresist, helping to create incredibly detailed patterns. These patterns are not just pretty designs; they outline every electronic component on the chip, from transistors to capacitors, all working together to perform the many tasks we often take for granted.

Once the UV light shines on the photomask, the exposed parts of the photoresist undergo a chemical change, making them either washable or resistant to a developer solution. After this exposure, the wafer gets treated with a developer that removes the washable areas, leaving behind a sharp pattern of hardened photoresist that closely resembles the original design. This creative process is a blend of art and engineering, resulting in a substrate that is ready for the next steps, like etching and doping, which will eventually lead to a fully functional microchip.

So, why is precision so important in this process? The answer is tied to the constant drive for miniaturization in the semiconductor industry. As technology evolves, the need for smaller, faster, and more efficient chips increases. Each new generation of microchips aims for smaller features, often measured in nanometers. To give you an idea, a human hair is about 80,000 to 100,000 nanometers wide. Photolithography needs to achieve incredible precision to ensure that these features are not only tiny but also correctly aligned and replicated throughout multiple layers of a chip. Even a tiny mistake or defect can ruin the functionality of the microchip, leading to failures that can be disastrous in critical situations.

The process of photolithography isn't just about exposure; it involves managing many factors that can affect the outcome. Engineers must carefully control aspects like exposure time, light intensity, and the optical properties of the materials used. Any slight variation can lead to issues in the final product, which is why modern photolithography equipment includes advanced monitoring systems. These systems help guarantee that the process stays within the strict tolerances necessary for the industry.

One more interesting thing about photolithography is the idea of resolution. The ability to create smaller features on a chip is largely determined by the wavelength of light used in the process. Over the years, the semiconductor industry has used various wavelengths, with deep ultraviolet (DUV) and extreme ultraviolet (EUV) light taking the lead recently. This move to shorter wavelengths has made it possible to produce incredibly intricate patterns, pushing the boundaries of microchip technology while keeping up with the fast-paced tech world.

Photolithography doesn't happen in a vacuum. It's part of a larger system involving many different players, including chip designers, equipment makers, and materials suppliers. Working together is crucial to make sure the process is efficient and keeps progressing. Innovation is a key part of this industry; new methods and technologies are always being developed to improve capabilities and cut costs in chip manufacturing.

One exciting innovation is the use of multiple patterning techniques, which allow manufacturers to double or even quadruple the number of features created in each exposure cycle. This method helps to overcome some of the challenges posed by traditional photolithography and opens up new possibilities for achieving desired feature sizes. By using techniques like self-aligned double patterning (SADP) and multiple patterning lithography, engineers can push the limits of what's possible further than ever before.

Moreover, the art of photolithography goes beyond just functionality; it captures the essence of creativity in technology. Each chip design is not just a technical project; it represents human ingenuity and imagination. Engineers, scientists, and designers work together to craft these intricate masterpieces, which ultimately enhance our lives in ways we might not fully understand.

Truly, the influence of microchips, created through photolithography, is felt in every corner of modern life. As we dive deeper into the Internet of Things (IoT), smart devices, and artificial intelligence (AI), the need for more advanced and powerful chips continues to grow. With each new wave in chip design and manufacturing, the significance of photolithography becomes even clearer. It's the gateway through which innovation flows, enabling the technological advances that shape our time.

As we explore the details of microchip production, we must recognize the role of photolithography as both a technical and artistic field. Mastering this process requires not only a strong grasp of physics and chemistry but also an appreciation for design and functionality. Balancing these elements will shape the future of technology and, in turn, our lives.

Creating the Photomask

Photomasks are the unsung heroes of microchip manufacturing, often overlooked in favor of their flashier counterparts in the photolithography process. However, without these precisely crafted templates, the delicate dance of light and material that creates microchips would simply not happen. At first glance, a photomask may seem like just a plain glass plate with a pattern on it, but it's actually a complex and crucial part of how our modern electronic devices are built.

These photomasks act as the blueprints for a microchip's design, guiding the light exposure that turns silicon wafers into functional, intricately designed chips. Think of them like the conductor of an orchestra, making sure each instrument plays perfectly in tune with the others. When UV light passes through the mask, it creates a detailed pattern on the photoresist layer, allowing tiny features like transistors and capacitors to be etched onto the wafer.

To truly appreciate photomasks, we need to recognize how unique they are. Each one is crafted with extreme care to match the exact specifications of a microchip design. Even the smallest mistakes can lead to huge problems. The industry demands an incredible level of precision; it's not just about getting the size right, but also about making sure the whole design holds together from the very first light exposure to the finished product. In a world where a nanometer can change everything, photomasks stand as guardians of design accuracy.

Just like a sculptor relies on their chisel to create a masterpiece, engineers depend on photomasks to bring their intricate designs to life. This is where the art of photomask design comes into play, requiring a sharp eye for detail and a solid understanding of both the technology and the science of light.

Creating a photomask is a team effort, often involving a mix of engineers, designers, and software experts. This collaboration ensures that every part of the microchip design is accurately represented. Specialized software is used to create the complex patterns that will make up the photomask. These tools help visualize how the final pattern will look when transferred to silicon, as well as how different light wavelengths will interact with the mask and the photoresist. This understanding is crucial when aiming for precision at such a tiny scale.

The design journey isn't a straight line; it's more of a winding path that involves making changes and adjustments as ideas develop and new challenges arise. Every tweak to the design is examined closely to see how it impacts the final product, making teamwork and communication essential. This collaboration results in a photomask that best captures the original microchip design, ready to guide the light that will shape the future of technology.

Once the design is set, the next step is making the photomask, which involves a careful manufacturing process. The base usually consists of a thin glass substrate that must be clear enough for ultraviolet light while being tough enough for the demands of photolithography. On top of this substrate, a light-sensitive layer called emulsion is applied. This emulsion will later be exposed to light in a controlled way to create the patterns needed for chip production.

Quality control is crucial during this production phase. Just like an artist inspects their canvas for flaws before they begin painting, engineers must meticulously check the photomasks for defects. Even tiny scratches, dust, or any other imperfections could cause major issues when the mask is used in the photolithography process. The industry uses advanced techniques to inspect for defects. High-resolution imaging systems and automated inspection tools are essential for spotting any problems, ensuring that only the best-quality photomasks make it to the production stage.

Maintaining the integrity of photomasks is incredibly important. Once they are made, these masks need careful handling, controlled storage, and regular inspections throughout their lifespan. Much like a treasured piece of art, a photomask can be easily damaged if not treated with care, and restoring it requires a meticulous process that demands both skill and patience. This comparison highlights not only how fragile photomasks can be, but also the artistry involved in creating them.

In today's fast-moving tech world, there's a constant push for innovation in photomask technology. New materials and manufacturing methods are making photomasks more durable and effective than ever. Developments like high-contrast materials and advanced patterning techniques are improving the resolution and functionality of photomasks. The shift towards new materials that can handle the demands of modern photolithography isn't just a trend; it's a necessity.

For example, new types of substrates can boost photomasks' performance in extreme ultraviolet (EUV) lithography, which uses shorter light wavelengths to achieve smaller feature sizes. These innovations not only enhance resolution but also extend the photomask's lifespan, ultimately lowering production costs.

Additionally, research into alternative designs, like phase-shifting masks, has come about as a way to improve the resolution capabilities of photomasks even further. These designs manipulate light waves to provide greater control over the exposure process, pushing the limits of what's possible in microchip design. As the industry advances, staying on the cutting edge of photomask technology is crucial for manufacturers who want to meet the growing demand for smaller, more efficient chips.

The world of photomasks is rich with complexity and significance, playing a key role in the microchip manufacturing process. As we explore the details of photomask creation, it becomes clear that these seemingly simple tools are actually the backbone of photolithography. They are the finely crafted templates that help engineers' designs come to life, precisely directing the light that shapes the future of technology.

The journey from design to mask isn't just a mechanical task; it's a blend of art, science, and innovation. Every photomask represents the teamwork of skilled individuals committed to expanding the possibilities in microchip technology. The story of photomasks is one of precision, quality, and an unwavering dedication to excellence, echoing the creative spirit that thrives in the realm of technological progress.

As we continue to dive into the details of microchip design and manufacturing, it becomes increasingly clear that photomasks are not just tools but vital pieces of a larger puzzle. They act as the bridge between dreams and reality, turning designers' visions into actual products that drive today's tech innovations. The art of creating photomasks is as crucial as the designs themselves, paving the way for a future that is more intricate and interconnected than ever before.

Multi-Layer Masking

Microchip design has come a long way, turning into a complex process that's much like a layered cake—each layer adds its own unique touch to the final creation. At the heart of this intricate engineering is the idea of multi-layer masking, a vital part of making advanced microchips. As the demand for smaller, faster, and more powerful chips grows, engineers turn to multi-layer masking to handle the complexity of designs filled with interconnected components.

To get a better grasp of multi-layer masking, think of a sprawling city seen from above. Each layer of buildings represents different parts of the microchip, while the roads connecting them symbolize the pathways that allow these parts to communicate. Just like a city needs careful planning to ensure everything fits together nicely, microchip designs require precise layering of circuitry. Each layer needs to be designed just right and lined up perfectly with the others to work well. This complexity is what makes multi-layer masking a significant challenge in chip design.

The process of multi-layer masking starts with making individual photomasks for each layer of the chip. Each photomask acts like a blueprint, directing where light will shine to expose the photoresist on the silicon wafer. You can imagine these masks as stencils used when decorating a cake. Each stencil must be crafted perfectly to ensure the finished product has all the right details. When these masks are stacked together, they create a complete structure that determines how the chip will function.

But the real challenge isn't just in creating these masks; it's in getting them aligned just right. Aligning them is like putting together a jigsaw puzzle—if even one piece is off, the picture won't look right. In microchip manufacturing, even a tiny misalignment—measured in nanometers—can cause serious issues. A misaligned layer could lead to short circuits or disconnects, potentially making the chip non-functional. So, achieving precise alignment isn't just a technical requirement; it's a fundamental principle that supports the entire microchip manufacturing process.

Precision alignment techniques are the unsung heroes in the world of multi-layer masking. One common method is optical proximity correction (OPC), which tweaks the designs on the photomasks to counteract the distortions that happen during the lithography process. Think of OPC as a ship's navigator, steering it safely through tricky waters that could otherwise send it off course. By predicting and correcting how patterns will change during exposure, OPC helps make sure the final product stays true to the original design.

Another useful tool for ensuring precise alignment is the use of alignment marks. These are special patterns placed on the silicon wafer that act as reference points for aligning each layer. It's similar to how a builder uses a plumb line to ensure a wall is straight. Alignment marks serve as visual guides, allowing equipment to adjust and position each mask with exceptional precision. Together, OPC and alignment marks create a strong system that boosts the reliability of multi-layer masking, giving engineers some peace of mind amid the daunting task of design.

Even with these clever techniques, alignment challenges persist. As microchip designs shrink, the allowable margin for alignment error becomes much smaller. A slight misalignment might be manageable in larger circuits, but at nanometer scales, there's hardly any room for error. This issue is made worse by variations in material properties, environmental factors, and the limitations of equipment. Each of these factors can introduce tiny mistakes that, when multiplied across several layers, can lead to serious problems.

The consequences of these challenges go beyond the manufacturing floor. As microchips become essential in everything from smartphones to complex computing systems, the stakes are incredibly high. A faulty chip could cause a critical system failure in anything from a self-driving car to a medical device or an aerospace application. This means that engineers not only have to design chips with intricate details, but they must also ensure that they're produced with unwavering accuracy.

To highlight the importance of multi-layer masking, consider the high-performance microchips used in today's advanced devices. Modern smartphones are engineering marvels, packed with features that require detailed chip designs. Each layer of the chip must work together seamlessly, enabling quick processing, efficient power use, and strong connectivity. If even one layer runs into trouble, it can affect the entire user experience.

Top technology companies are developing smart solutions to tackle the alignment hurdles posed by multi-layer masking. For example, they've created advanced metrology tools that use lasers and imaging technology to confirm that each layer is positioned correctly. These high-tech systems can measure the spaces between layers with incredible accuracy, allowing for real-time adjustments that keep the manufacturing process running smoothly.

Moreover, some organizations are now turning to machine learning and artificial intelligence to improve their alignment processes. By studying historical data and using predictive algorithms, these technologies can spot potential misalignment problems before they arise, allowing engineers to make adjustments ahead of time. This data-driven approach not only helps streamline production but also reduces the chances of defects, ensuring that the end products meet the high standards expected by the market.

The impact of multi-layer masking reaches far beyond smartphones, influencing various areas of technology. In the automotive industry, for instance, multi-layer masked chips are crucial for creating sophisticated driver-assistance systems. These systems rely on a network of sensors and processors to analyze data from the vehicle's surroundings, making split-second decisions that can affect safety. Each chip in these systems must operate without a hitch, as any error caused by misalignment could have serious repercussions.

In healthcare, advanced medical devices like imaging equipment and diagnostic tools increasingly depend on precision-engineered microchips. These chips need to perform reliably to ensure accurate diagnoses and effective treatments. The role of multi-layer masking in these applications is vital; it forms the foundation for safe and effective medical technology.

As demand for wearable technology continues to rise, multi-layer masking is also key in producing microchips that power these devices. From smartwatches to fitness trackers, these gadgets need complex chips that can do many things while staying compact. The precision provided by multi-layer masking allows manufacturers to fit more functions into smaller devices, catering to consumers who want efficiency and convenience.

In the end, the world of multi-layer masking is one of constant innovation and change. As technology progresses, so do the methods used to design and produce microchips. Engineers and researchers are always on the lookout for new materials and techniques to enhance the performance of multi-layer masks. For example, the development of advanced polymers is leading to greater durability and accuracy in photomasks. These improvements not only make the manufacturing process better but also help create more advanced and capable microchips.

As we explore the complexities of multi-layer masking, it's clear that precision is at the heart of microchip manufacturing. Each layer of masking brings us closer to realizing the technological dreams that shape our world today. The commitment to excellence in this field is steadfast, and the teamwork among engineers, designers, and technicians is evident. Together, they are building the future, ensuring that every chip produced reflects the artistry and creativity of human innovation.

In this intricate dance of design and production, multi-layer masking serves as a reminder that even in the most complicated systems, the little details truly matter. The journey from concept to silicon may be filled with challenges, but it also holds great promise for what's to come. As we continue to push technological boundaries, the significance of precision in multi-layer masking will remain a guiding principle, lighting the way towards a future where the capabilities of microchips can only be limited by our imagination.

Chapter 6: The Fabrication Factory

Semiconductor Fabrication Plants

When we think about the technology that powers our everyday devices, we often forget about the intricate processes that create microchips. At the very heart of this technological marvel are semiconductor fabrication plants—places where the building blocks of our digital world come to life. To many, these facilities might seem like cold, sterile spaces filled with machinery and materials, but they are so much more. They feel like high-tech laboratories, buzzing with innovation and precision, where every detail is carefully managed to ensure the creation of perfect microchips.

The heart of these fabrication plants is the cleanroom, a space designed to minimize contamination. Picture stepping into a room where the air is filtered and purified to levels you would rarely find outside a hospital. The idea of "clean" in the semiconductor world goes way beyond our everyday understanding. Dust, hair, moisture, and even a person's breath can introduce tiny particles that can ruin the delicate structure of a microchip. Cleanrooms are like the operating rooms of technology, with air quality measured in parts per billion and surfaces scrubbed to an almost obsessive level.

Entering a cleanroom requires a transformation; workers don special outfits that look a bit like what astronauts wear. This gear—coveralls, booties, gloves, and face masks—serves two purposes: it keeps the workers safe and prevents them from accidentally contaminating the space. While this might seem like overkill, in a world where even the smallest speck can ruin a chip, it's absolutely necessary. Staff members go through rigorous training to familiarize themselves with the rules of these pristine environments, learning to move gracefully and carefully, almost as if they're part of a choreographed dance.

All this effort focuses on one goal: creating the most efficient and reliable microchips possible. Inside these plants, silicon wafers—thin slices of silicon that form the base of microchips—undergo a series of complex steps to become the powerful processors that drive our smartphones, laptops, and many other devices. The journey from raw silicon to finished product involves multiple intricate processes, each more vital than the last.

But the complexity of fabrication doesn't stop with the physical environment. The logistics of running a semiconductor fabrication plant are remarkable in their own right. These facilities operate around the clock, with teams of engineers, technicians, and operators working together in a highly coordinated effort. Every step of the process, from receiving raw materials to delivering completed chips, is carefully scheduled and monitored. Timing is so crucial that a delay in one part of the process can lead to significant setbacks.

Imagine the careful choreography needed to ensure that silicon wafers are processed on time: they must move from one machine to another, often going through hundreds of processing steps. Each step relies on the previous one, and even a minor hiccup in scheduling can lead to lost time and wasted materials. The complexity of this dance is heightened by the fact that semiconductor technology operates at the cutting edge of physics and engineering. As the demand for faster, more efficient chips rises, the details of fabrication must adapt to keep up.

The demand for microchips has surged in recent years, driven by advancements in everything from artificial intelligence to the ever-growing Internet of Things. This spike in demand has pushed semiconductor fabrication plants to their limits, prompting them to innovate not just in technology but also in how they operate. Companies are pouring millions into building new facilities and automating existing ones, incorporating robotics and artificial intelligence to streamline processes and cut down on human error.

Moreover, the semiconductor industry is famous for its ups and downs, with periods of boom and bust that can leave companies scrambling to keep up. When demand is high, plants run at full capacity, operating equipment non-stop to meet orders. During slow periods, they must find ways to scale back without compromising their standards. This balancing act showcases the industry's volatility and the skill needed to navigate it.

Safety is a top priority in these fabrication plants. Working with materials used in microchip production can be risky, so protecting workers is crucial. Cleanrooms are designed not only to limit contamination but also to ensure the safety of the people inside. Air pressure is carefully managed to keep outside contaminants out, and workers must follow strict protocols before entering. This helps create an environment that is as safe as possible, allowing them to concentrate on their work.

Beyond the physical and safety challenges, there's a human side to semiconductor fabrication that often gets overshadowed by technology. The workers in these plants are skilled professionals, often with years of specialized training. They are problem solvers, constantly troubleshooting the challenges that arise during microchip production. Their work demands great patience and keen attention to detail since one small mistake can lead to significant issues in the final products.

Importantly, these workers are part of a larger global ecosystem. The semiconductor supply chain is complex and wide-ranging, crossing borders and continents. Raw materials come from various regions, and the finished products often end up in devices made in entirely different places. This interconnectedness highlights that semiconductor fabrication plants are not just local operations; they are essential parts of a vast global industry.

In this fast-paced era of technological advancement, semiconductor fabrication plants are at the cutting edge of innovation. They embody the blend of engineering skill and technological creativity, turning the amazing designs of microchips into real products that shape our daily lives.

As we take a closer look at the processes within these facilities, from etching to deposition and beyond, it becomes clear that the story of microchips is not just about the technology itself, but also about the dedicated people and sophisticated environments that make this technology possible. Each microchip is a testament to human creativity, crafted in a place that blends artistry with science.

All in all, the world of semiconductor fabrication is a fascinating mix of cleanliness, precision, innovation, and teamwork. It's a complex web of human effort and technological progress, all coming together to create the microchips that support our modern lives. The next time you pick up your smartphone or turn on your computer, take a moment to appreciate the hidden world of semiconductor fabrication plants—the unseen factories that drive our digital age. While these facilities may not be visible to most, their influence is felt in every aspect of our world.

Etching and Deposition Processes

Picture this: a blank canvas, a fresh, unmarked surface just waiting for an artist's brush to turn it into something extraordinary. In the realm of semiconductor fabrication, that canvas is a silicon wafer, a thin slice of silicon that serves as the foundation for the intricate designs powering our digital devices. But before any of those circuits and pathways can come alive, a process known as etching must happen—it's a technique that creates patterns and features on a microscopic scale. Think of etching like using a stencil to make a beautiful design on paper; both demand precision, patience, and a solid understanding of how materials work together.

The etching process kicks off with photolithography, a technique that's somewhat similar to photography itself. Just as a photographer captures an image on film, photolithography uses light to carve a pattern onto the silicon wafer. A light-sensitive chemical called photoresist is spread over the wafer's surface, forming a coating that reacts when exposed to ultraviolet light. Next, the wafer is placed under a mask that holds the desired pattern—imagine it as a stencil. When light shines through the mask onto the photoresist, it changes the chemical makeup of the areas that come into contact with the light.

Once the exposure is complete, the wafer goes through a developing process. The areas of photoresist that were exposed to light either become more or less soluble, depending on the type of photoresist used. This selective solubility allows for detailed patterns to form on the wafer—patterns that will eventually guide the etching process that follows. The outcome is a visual version of the chip's design, primed for the next step in production.

When etching starts, it's crucial to recognize that there are two main methods:

wet etching and dry etching. Each technique has its own advantages and is suited for different needs. Wet etching uses liquid chemicals to take layers off the silicon wafer, much like washing away dirt with soap and water. This method is usually quicker and can create smooth surfaces, but it isn't without its drawbacks. Wet etching tends to be isotropic, which means it etches both vertically and horizontally at the same time. This can lead to undercutting, where the etching solution erodes the material beneath the photoresist, potentially causing unexpected issues in the final design.

On the flip side, dry etching offers greater precision. This method uses gases or plasmas to remove material from the wafer. By maintaining a controlled environment, dry etching can be highly directional, removing material in straight lines while minimizing undercutting. Imagine a sculptor carefully chiseling away at a block of stone, removing only the parts that aren't needed to reveal a beautiful figure underneath. Dry etching acts as the sculptor in the semiconductor world, providing the control needed to create features that are often only nanometers wide.

As we dive into these etching techniques, it becomes clear just how important precision is in this process. Even the tiniest mistakes can lead to major differences in the chip's performance. An error as small as a few nanometers can disrupt the flow of electricity through the circuits, ultimately resulting in a faulty chip. In the semiconductor industry, where the margin for error is incredibly slim, paying close attention to detail is vital. Those working in fabrication plants must be not only skilled technicians but also intuitive thinkers who understand how each step impacts the next.

Once etching has revealed the intricate designs on the silicon wafer, the focus shifts to the deposition processes. This stage is much like layering clothing or frosting a cake, where various materials are carefully added to the wafer to build the necessary structures. These layers form the complex architectures found in modern microchips—structures that will eventually hold transistors, capacitors, and other components essential for processing and storing information.

The two main deposition techniques used in semiconductor fabrication are physical vapor deposition (PVD) and chemical vapor deposition (CVD). Let's explore these to see how they help build the final product.

Physical vapor deposition is a graceful technique that involves changing materials from a solid to a vapor, which then condenses onto the silicon wafer. Imagine putting a handful of ice in a warm room; as it melts into water, the vapor rises and eventually condenses elsewhere. In PVD, materials like metals are heated until they turn into vapor, creating a thin film that coats the wafer. The result is a uniform layer that sticks to the intended areas, forming the foundation for the next steps.

In contrast, chemical vapor deposition takes a different approach to layering. In CVD, various gaseous chemicals are introduced into the chamber housing the silicon wafer. At higher temperatures, these gases react chemically, resulting in solid material being deposited onto the wafer's surface. CVD is often used for creating high-quality insulating layers and has the added perk of evenly coating complex structures. Think of it like frosting a multi-layered cake—ensuring that every nook and cranny is filled and every contour is smoothed out.

As these layers accumulate, the artistry of chip creation becomes clear. Each layer has its specific role and must be applied with precision that would impress even the most talented chef. Finding the perfect balance of materials, temperatures, and timing is essential for achieving optimal chip performance. Just like a well-crafted recipe yields a delicious dish, the careful application of etching and deposition processes leads to the powerful microchips that drive our technology.

At this point, it's good to recognize that the semiconductor industry is always changing. New materials and innovative techniques are constantly being developed to push the limits of what's possible in chip design. Researchers and engineers continually search for ways to boost microchip performance while shrinking their size—an effort that has led to increasingly complex designs and architectures.

As the industry evolves, the significance of etching and deposition processes stays crucial. They form the backbone of semiconductor fabrication, the stages that transform raw silicon into the intricate, highly functional components we depend on every day. By understanding these processes, we gain a deeper appreciation for the sophisticated machinery and techniques behind our devices, as well as the dedicated individuals who make it all happen.

So, the next time you find yourself marveling at your smartphone or laptop, remember that its heart—the microchip—is the product of countless hours of precise work involving intricate etching and deposition processes. These aren't just technical steps in manufacturing; they represent an art form of their own, blending science and creativity to produce the powerful technology that shapes our modern world. The story of microchips is one of ingenuity, innovation, and human effort, showing just how closely intertwined technology and creativity can be.

Doping and Activation

Imagine a peaceful, clear lake, its surface mirroring the sky above. This serene scene is similar to pure silicon, a key material at the heart of our microchip technology. Silicon has a remarkable ability to conduct electricity, but in its pure state, it can only do so to a limited degree. To turn this simple element into a powerful player in the semiconductor world, we need to add a little something extra, much like adding a dash of salt to a dish: we need to dope it.

Doping is when we intentionally mix impurities into pure silicon, changing its electrical properties and letting it show its true potential. Think of it as a form of culinary magic—just as a pinch of salt can elevate the taste of food, doping boosts silicon's ability to conduct electricity. Without this crucial step, silicon would sit quietly on the sidelines of electronics, unable to handle the demanding tasks it performs in our devices.

At its core, doping is a way to create two different types of silicon that behave quite differently when it comes to electricity: n-type and p-type. Both are essential for semiconductor devices, and knowing how they differ helps us understand how microchips function.

N-type doping is like adding more players to a game, increasing the energy and excitement. In this case, we introduce elements from group V of the periodic table, such as phosphorus or arsenic, into the silicon structure. These dopants have five valence electrons compared to silicon's four. When they bond with silicon atoms, four of the dopant's electrons form covalent bonds with neighboring silicon atoms, while the fifth one is free. This extra electron is a game changer—it boosts the electron concentration in the silicon, making it better at conducting electricity.

On the other side, p-type doping takes a different route, creating vacancies like empty seats in our game, inviting holes to join instead of more players. Here, we use elements from group III of the periodic table, like boron or aluminum. These elements have only three valence electrons. When they're added to the silicon lattice, they bond with silicon atoms but leave behind a "hole" where an electron is missing. This absence encourages neighboring electrons to move in and fill the gap, creating a flow of positive charge carriers, or holes, that help to conduct electricity.

The shift from pure silicon to n-type and p-type silicon isn't just a surface change; it fundamentally alters the material's electrical properties, making it possible to create diodes, transistors, and integrated circuits—the building blocks of modern electronics. These doping types are crucial for forming the "p-n junction," where n-type and p-type materials meet. This junction is at the heart of many semiconductor devices, allowing us to control and direct electrical current in ways that power our smartphones, computers, and more.

The methods used in doping—ion implantation and diffusion—are vital for getting the results we want. Ion implantation, as the name suggests, involves firing ions of the chosen dopant into the silicon wafer. These ions embed themselves in the silicon structure. Precision is key here; controlling the energy and amount of ions is essential to ensure everything is uniform and achieves the desired doping profile. This technique allows for very specific doping profiles, fine-tuning the electrical properties of the silicon with great accuracy.

On the other hand, the diffusion method takes a different approach. In this technique, the silicon wafer is placed in a furnace with a gas or solid source of the dopant. As the temperature rises, the dopant atoms spread into the silicon lattice over time. This method can create broader doping profiles, which might be useful in certain situations. However, it offers less control compared to ion implantation since the diffusion process depends on time, temperature, and concentration levels.

After the doping processes, we reach a crucial stage known as activation. This is where everything comes together. The dopants need to become electrically active and truly join the silicon matrix. Simply inserting them isn't enough; they must be in a state where they can help conduct electricity.

Activation often involves a post-doping heating step, where the silicon wafer is heated to high temperatures—usually hundreds of degrees Celsius. This heat helps the dopants settle into the right spots in the lattice and reduces any defects that may have occurred during doping. It's like rolling out the red carpet for those dopants, allowing them to blend in and become part of the silicon family. Once activated, the dopants significantly enhance the conductivity of the silicon, making sure the microchip can perform its functions.

The importance of doping and activation goes far beyond just individual microchips. As technology continues to advance, the need for smaller, faster, and more efficient devices grows stronger. The techniques and processes related to doping play a key role in this evolution. By controlling conductivity at the atomic level, we can fit more transistors into smaller spaces, enhancing performance while cutting down on power use.

Just think about how much progress we've made in a few decades. Microchips that used to fill entire rooms can now fit in the palm of your hand, containing billions of transistors. This remarkable change wouldn't have been possible without advancements in doping and activation processes, which have allowed engineers to stretch the limits of what we can achieve, fueling the rapid technological evolution we experience today.

Looking ahead, the challenges in doping for semiconductor technology keep changing. With new materials like gallium nitride and silicon carbide on the rise, researchers are exploring new doping strategies to tap into their unique properties. The aim is to boost performance and efficiency in applications that demand higher power and thermal stability. Doping is no longer a one-size-fits-all process; it must adapt and innovate to keep up with an ever-evolving landscape.

In the semiconductor world, doping is more than just a technical detail—it's a foundation for innovation that allows us to combine functionality and performance seamlessly. It showcases human creativity, where the careful addition of a few specific elements can unleash fantastic potential. Each time we use our devices, we enjoy the results of this meticulous work, reminding us that behind their sleek designs lies a complex world of science and artistry.

So, the next time you make a call on your smartphone or stream a video on your tablet, take a moment to appreciate the intricate dance of electrons and holes that makes it all possible. Behind the scenes, the world of doping and activation works tirelessly, ensuring our technology runs smoothly and efficiently. This quiet yet powerful process is the unsung hero of the semiconductor industry—often hidden from view but absolutely crucial for the functionality we sometimes take for granted.

Ethan Maxwell

Chapter 7: Testing and Quality Assurance

Initial Testing Phases

In the world of microchip manufacturing, transforming raw silicon into a fully functional chip is a detailed and careful process. When we first step into the initial testing phases, we find ourselves at a point where the very first check-up of silicon wafers takes place. These wafers are the building blocks of microchips. Although they are delicate, they carry a great deal of potential. They are the unsung heroes—thin slices of silicon that have gone through rigorous processes to reach this stage. Now it's time to evaluate whether they're ready for the demanding tech environment ahead.

Think of the initial inspection of silicon wafers as a health check-up for an athlete before a big game. It's vital to ensure there aren't any flaws that could affect their performance later on. Engineers and technicians use various methods for this inspection, each one designed to uncover potential issues that might compromise the quality of the chips. One of the standout techniques is optical inspection, a key player in the fight against defects.

Optical inspection uses strong light sources and advanced imaging systems to magnify the wafer's surface, revealing tiny details that would be invisible to the naked eye. This method works by shining light on the wafer and capturing the reflections and patterns that emerge. Technicians carefully analyze these images, searching for signs of scratches, dirt, or other impurities that could lead to failure. The precision of optical inspection is impressive; it can spot defects as small as just a few microns. To put that in perspective, a single micron is one-millionth of a meter. While these tiny flaws may seem insignificant to most, in the microchip world, even the smallest imperfection can lead to major failures, rendering the chip useless.

But that's not all—there's also scanning electron microscopy (SEM), which takes the inspection to a whole new level. Think of SEM as giving engineers a super high-powered magnifying glass to examine the atomic structure of the silicon. This technique uses electron beams instead of light to create incredibly detailed images of the wafer's surface. It provides a three-dimensional view that reveals not only surface defects but also structural issues that could impact performance. Engineers can spot problems like contamination, irregularities in the crystal structure, and other hidden flaws that could threaten the chip's functionality.

To keep up high-quality standards, it's critical to understand the kinds of imperfections that can happen during the wafer fabrication process. For example, particulate contamination is a common enemy in this field. Even the smallest speck of dust or oil can disrupt the delicate processes that follow. These little particles can cause electrical shorts, impact the chip's performance, or even lead to complete failure. Engineers know this potential risk all too well, working diligently to catch these flaws early before they turn into larger headaches in later production stages.

As inspections continue, we can't overlook yield analysis, a key aspect that acts as a gauge for the manufacturing process. Yield, in the context of microchip production, refers to the percentage of functional chips produced from a single wafer. A higher yield means not only an efficient manufacturing process but also a clear sign that the initial testing phases have worked well. It reflects the overall health of the manufacturing environment and shows that the company is staying competitive, especially in an industry with razor-thin margins.

Yield analysis is more than just crunching numbers; it's a careful balance of data and decision-making. Engineers gather information on how many good chips were produced versus defective ones and use statistical methods to evaluate this information. They look for trends over time, searching for patterns that can guide adjustments to the fabrication process. For instance, if the yield for a specific batch of wafers drops below expectations, it raises a red flag. Engineers analyze the data, identify possible sources of failure, and then make informed decisions to address the issue.

Picture this: a manufacturer discovers that a specific production run yielded far fewer functional chips than expected. This could happen for various reasons—maybe there was a problem with the equipment or inconsistencies in the raw materials. By examining the yield data, engineers can trace back through the manufacturing steps to find out what went wrong. They might uncover that a specific lot of silicon had impurities or that a machine used in the photolithography process wasn't properly calibrated. Each detail is a clue in a larger puzzle, and effectively analyzing yield empowers companies to continuously improve their processes.

The impact of yield analysis goes beyond the production line; it affects the entire organization. A company that achieves higher yields can lower costs, boost profits, and invest in future innovations. On the flip side, a decline in yield can create resource strain, backlogs, and dissatisfaction among customers who rely on timely deliveries. It's a high-stakes situation where every chip counts, and maintaining a steady yield is crucial.

This dedication to quality assurance doesn't just start and end on the factory floor. It's clear that the initial testing phases lay the groundwork for everything that comes next. By investing the necessary time and effort upfront, manufacturers can reduce defects and enhance yields, ensuring that the chips that reach the market are reliable and perform as expected. The details of these initial inspections reflect the hard work and foresight of engineers who recognize that the quality of silicon wafers directly impacts the performance of the devices they power.

As we navigate this intricate landscape, it becomes evident that the initial testing phases of silicon wafers are fundamental to the entire microchip manufacturing process. The thorough examination of wafers, the use of advanced inspection methods, and the careful analysis of yield data all work together to achieve the ultimate goal of delivering high-quality microchips. The tech world is unforgiving, and the stakes are incredibly high. Yet, in the capable hands of skilled engineers and technicians, these initial testing phases stand strong against the flaws that could threaten the complex systems we depend on daily.

In a realm where microchips are the backbone of innovation, the importance of these early testing phases is undeniable. They're not just a formality; they're a vital step in making sure that the microchips we use in everything from smartphones to electric vehicles are built to last. As we continue to explore the diverse world of microchip manufacturing, it becomes clear that the commitment to quality assurance doesn't fade; instead, it grows and adapts to the challenges of a fast-evolving technological landscape.

Functional Testing

After engineers have meticulously examined silicon wafers to ensure there are no flaws that could undermine their future performance, we move into the exciting world of functional testing. Think of this stage as a rite of passage for microchips, where they transform from mere potential into reliable components ready to take on real-world tasks. Just like athletes go through rigorous physical exams to prove they are fit to compete, microchips must also show they can handle their designated jobs seamlessly, even in varying conditions.

Functional testing is much more than just checking items off a list; it's a detailed process that confirms every chip does exactly what it's meant to do. During this phase, chips are put through a battery of tests that examine their performance, durability, and overall functionality. Testing isn't just a one-time event—it's a series of evaluations that explore every possible aspect of how a chip operates. The stakes are high because even the tiniest failure can lead to significant issues later on, impacting everything from consumer gadgets to essential infrastructure.

At the core of functional testing is performance testing, which is crucial for measuring how well a chip can perform its tasks. You can think of performance testing like a decathlon for microchips, rigorously testing speed, power usage, and overall capability. During this phase, engineers create various scenarios to push the chip to its limits. Performance testing isn't for the faint-hearted; it's where chips are stressed, strained, and subjected to some of the toughest conditions imaginable.

One of the toughest parts of performance testing is stress testing, where chips are pushed to their extremes to see how they behave under harsh conditions. For example, if a chip is designed to work best within a specific temperature range, engineers may crank up the heat or plunge it into freezing temperatures to observe its reaction.

Does it keep performing well? Does it slow down? Or does it just stop working? Even well-established chips can surprise us—sometimes in frightening ways—when faced with these high-pressure situations. The goal is to find that breaking point, ensuring that once deployed in real-world settings, the chip will perform consistently without any hitches.

Power consumption is another vital aspect of performance testing. In an age where energy efficiency is key, chips that use up too much power aren't just unwanted; they can be unsustainable. Engineers carefully assess how much energy a chip uses, making sure it operates efficiently without sacrificing performance. Chips that are power-hungry can overheat and wear out sooner than expected, so finding the ideal balance between power use and performance is crucial. As technology advances, the need for energy-efficient microchips grows stronger, making power consumption testing a top priority during the design phase.

Alongside performance testing, environmental testing adds another layer of reassurance. This is where chips are subjected to different external conditions to mimic the environments they will eventually face. Environmental testing looks at a wide range of factors, including changes in temperature, humidity, vibrations, and electromagnetic interference. Each of these factors presents unique challenges that can impact a chip's reliability.

For example, take an automotive microchip that needs to work properly under the hood of a car. This chip will be exposed to extreme temperatures and vibrations while also facing moisture and other pollutants. If it can't handle these conditions, it could jeopardize vehicle performance, safety, and reliability. Environmental testing ensures that chips not only survive these challenges but thrive, functioning reliably regardless of what obstacles come their way.

Humidity testing is especially important for chips used in consumer electronics, which might encounter less-than-ideal conditions. Excess moisture can cause chips to malfunction or degrade, leading to failures in devices where reliability is critical. By simulating high humidity, engineers can check whether the chip remains functional under such stresses.

Vibration testing is another crucial part of environmental testing, especially for chips designed for industries like aerospace and automotive. During these tests, chips are subjected to mechanical vibrations that mirror real-world conditions. Engineers closely monitor how the chip performs during these trials to ensure it can withstand the demands of its intended environment. A chip that fails during vibration tests could cause major problems in systems where precision and reliability are essential.

Then there's electromagnetic interference (EMI) testing, which is key for making sure chips can operate without being disrupted by external electromagnetic fields. In our world filled with wireless signals and electronic devices, interference is always possible. EMI testing simulates these conditions to see how chips react. Engineers look for any signs of performance issues, making sure the chip can work smoothly even amid the interference that modern technology brings.

The significance of environmental testing is hard to overstate, particularly in fields where reliability is critical. A chip meant for aerospace must work flawlessly at 30,000 feet, facing pressures and temperatures that would shock most electronics. Through thorough environmental testing, manufacturers can ensure they are providing chips that can withstand the real-world challenges ahead, ultimately leading to more trustworthy products.

As we explore this thorough assessment, it's important to remember that functional testing isn't just a one-time deal. It's an ongoing commitment throughout the chip's lifecycle. Manufacturers are dedicated to quality assurance, regularly revisiting testing methods as technology evolves, new materials are introduced, and manufacturing techniques improve. By continuously refining their testing processes, they can ensure their chips stay at the forefront of performance and reliability.

The feedback loop created by functional testing also plays a big role in product development. Engineers take careful notes on the results of performance and environmental tests, using this data to guide future designs. If a chip shows unexpected behavior during testing, it becomes a valuable learning moment. Engineers analyze the results to understand what went wrong and how to prevent similar issues in the future. This back-and-forth process not only improves the current product but also lays the groundwork for future innovations.

In today's fast-moving tech world, where consumer expectations are always rising, the importance of thorough functional testing is vital. It's a key part of the manufacturing process that guarantees microchips are ready to meet the demands of modern applications. As we rely more and more on these small powerhouses, manufacturers must be devoted to providing chips that meet—and even exceed—design expectations.

Ultimately, functional testing acts as a gatekeeper, ensuring only the highest quality microchips reach the market. Through comprehensive performance and environmental evaluations, engineers can be confident that the chips they produce can excel in a variety of conditions, delivering the dependable performance that consumers expect. The reliability of our technology depends on these testing protocols, and as microchip design evolves, so too must the strategies used to ensure their success.

As we take a step back to look at the landscape of functional testing, it's clear that this stage is more than just a formality; it's the foundation upon which high-quality microchip production relies. In our technology-driven world, where microchips play a crucial role in the devices that are now integral to our lives, ensuring their functionality is not just an option—it's a must. With every test run, engineers are not just protecting their products; they are also helping to push forward the technology that shapes our world.

Quality Control Measures

In the high-stakes world of microchip manufacturing, keeping quality at the forefront isn't just a box to check off; it's a steadfast promise that influences every part of the production process. This ongoing drive for excellence highlights the significance of quality assurance, which becomes a core part of designing and producing microchips. It evolves from simply inspecting the finished product into an everyday mindset. Producing a dependable microchip is much like creating a beautiful piece of art—every step in the process needs careful attention to ensure that the final product meets the highest standards.

At the core of constant quality control is a structured method that includes statistical process control (SPC) and strong feedback loops. These elements are vital for understanding how to keep the manufacturing process on track and make improvements over time. Think of SPC as a watchful guardian of production, examining data closely to catch any variations that could compromise quality. By using statistics to assess how manufacturing processes are performing, engineers can spot any deviations from the norm—much like a conductor ensuring an orchestra plays in harmony. When a process is out of tune, engineers step in to correct it before it causes major issues with the final product.

Introducing SPC isn't just about reacting to problems; it's a proactive way of creating a culture of ongoing improvement. It starts with setting control limits, which are the guidelines for acceptable performance in certain production processes. These limits are based on historical data and expected variability. By regularly gathering and examining data from the manufacturing floor, engineers can monitor performance in real-time, spotting trends and patterns that might signal upcoming problems.

For example, let's say a manufacturer is producing a batch of microchips that need to meet specific voltage requirements. With SPC, engineers can keep a close eye on the voltage readings from the production line. If they notice a gradual change suggesting the chips are drifting outside acceptable limits, they can quickly make adjustments—like recalibrating machinery or changing the input materials—stopping a wave of defective chips before it starts. This careful oversight guarantees that quality isn't an afterthought, but a key part of the production journey.

Another crucial part of quality control is creating feedback loops that take testing results and weave them into ongoing design and manufacturing practices. This cyclical process enables insights gained from testing to shape future designs, fostering a dynamic link between production and innovation. When chips go through thorough testing, the information gathered doesn't just fade away once the tests are done. Instead, it's carefully recorded and analyzed, becoming a valuable resource for future projects.

For instance, if a particular batch of chips shows inconsistent performance, engineers will dig into the data, looking closely at every detail to find the underlying cause. Was there an issue with the raw materials? Did something change in the manufacturing conditions? Or was it a mistake in the design? Once the problem is identified, this feedback goes back to the design team, who can tweak the specifications or adjust the manufacturing process. This loop of feedback and improvement ensures that lessons learned are put to good use, creating a culture of innovation that keeps growing.

Moreover, the role of quality assurance goes beyond just the technical side of production; it also shapes the overall attitude of the workforce. A company that emphasizes quality control builds a culture of accountability and pride among its workers. When team members realize that their efforts directly affect the reliability of the final product, they become more engaged in the process. They take ownership of their roles and work hard to uphold the high standards set by the organization. This shared sense of purpose unites the team in their quest for excellence.

To further illustrate this idea, consider how integrating cross-functional teams into the quality control process can enhance outcomes.

By bringing together engineers, designers, and production staff, companies can tap into different viewpoints to spot potential quality issues. In regular meetings, the team reviews testing data, discusses trends, and brainstorms solutions together. This collaborative approach fosters camaraderie and ensures that everyone's input is valued. Not only does this strengthen the quality of the microchips being produced, but it also creates a better work environment for everyone involved.

In the fast-paced world of microchip manufacturing, where technology is constantly advancing and consumer expectations are ever-increasing, the ability to adapt and uphold high-quality standards becomes more critical. As manufacturing processes change, so must the quality control measures that support them. Continuous training and education are key to making sure teams have the latest tools and knowledge to tackle quality issues as they pop up.

Organizations that invest in their employees through ongoing training sessions, workshops, and hands-on practice empower their teams to become advocates for quality. They learn to identify potential problems, understand statistical methods, and recognize the importance of thorough testing protocols. This way, quality control becomes a team effort, with everyone—from entry-level technicians to seasoned engineers—actively contributing to the mission of maintaining excellence.

As microchip technology progresses, new challenges will arise. For example, the trend toward smaller chips creates unique challenges in manufacturing precision. As components shrink and grow more intricate, even tiny variations in the production process can lead to significant failures. This means quality control measures must adapt and incorporate modern technologies like machine learning and data analytics to improve predictive capabilities.

By using sophisticated algorithms to analyze production data, manufacturers can find patterns and potential quality issues before they become serious problems. Predictive analytics can predict deviations from desired specifications, allowing real-time adjustments to the manufacturing process. This forward-thinking strategy not only boosts product quality but also reduces waste and cuts the costs associated with reworking or returning products.

As we explore the intricate world of microchip manufacturing, it's clear that quality control measures are not an afterthought; they are woven into every layer of the process. From statistical process control to proactive feedback loops, these practices form the backbone of a strong manufacturing system. By nurturing a culture of quality, investing in employee training, and embracing new technologies, organizations can not only meet but exceed the ever-increasing expectations of the market.

In the end, in the world of microchip production, quality control isn't just a set of practices; it's a guiding philosophy that ensures the reliability and performance of the technology that drives our modern lives. As we continue to depend on these tiny yet powerful components, it's vital that quality stays at the forefront of manufacturing efforts. Through a steadfast commitment to excellence, we can make sure that the microchips of tomorrow are built on a foundation of trust, reliability, and innovation.

Chapter 8: Packaging and Integration

Chip Packaging Basics

In the vast world of microchips, the design and manufacturing stages often steal the spotlight, but there's another key player that deserves recognition: packaging. While chip packaging may not receive the same admiration as the intricate circuits etched into silicon, it plays an essential role in the microchip story. Think of it as the protective shell that safeguards fragile components from the harsh realities of the outside world, ensuring these powerful little devices can smoothly fit into all the electronic gadgets we rely on daily.

Imagine chip packaging as similar to slipping your smartphone into a protective case. Just like a case protects against drops and scratches while still allowing you to use your phone, packaging shields microchips from heat, moisture, and physical harm. It's both an art and a science—a mix of engineering, materials science, and design that guarantees microchips don't just survive their environments but really thrive.

Chip packaging comes in different forms, each designed with specific performance and application needs in mind. The most common types include Dual In-line Package (DIP), Surface-Mount Device (SMD), Ball Grid Array (BGA), and Chip-on-Board (COB). Each of these packaging styles not only affects the microchip's durability but also plays a vital role in how well it operates.

DIP packages were some of the first packaging styles to hit the market. They're recognizable for their rectangular shape and two rows of pins. Popular during the 1970s and 1980s, their straightforward design made them a favorite among hobbyists and engineers. However, as technology advanced and the desire for smaller devices grew, the downsides of DIP became evident. The size of the package and the distance between the pins limited the number of connections, placing a cap on the chip's potential.

On the other hand, Surface-Mount Devices (SMD) represent a big step forward. With SMD, chips are mounted directly onto the surface of a printed circuit board (PCB), so there's no need for long pin connections. This change not only saves space but also boosts electrical performance. Thanks to SMD, manufacturers can fit more components into a smaller area, making it the go-to choice for today's consumer electronics. But there's a catch: handling and soldering these tiny packages can be tricky, especially for those used to the larger DIP.

Then we have the Ball Grid Array (BGA), which takes connection to the next level. Instead of pins, microchips in BGA packages come with solder balls arranged in a grid on the bottom. This setup allows for more connections in a smaller space, which is great for high-performance needs like graphics processing units and server processors. The downside? Assembling BGAs can be tricky. If the process isn't done with care, the microchip can end up misaligned during manufacturing, leading to unreliable connections and performance issues.

Chip-on-Board (COB) packaging offers an even more radical shift from traditional styles. In this method, the chip is directly bonded to the PCB, creating an ultra-compact design that can fit in spaces once thought impossible. COB is often used in applications where being small really matters, like in wearables. Although its compact nature is appealing, it does come with challenges for heat management. With fewer layers surrounding the chip, heat dissipation can become an issue, meaning creative cooling solutions might be needed.

When considering these packaging options, it's critical to look beyond just physical protection. You also need to think about thermal performance, electrical properties, and the overall reliability of the microchip in its specific application. Each packaging choice has its pros and cons, which can directly affect how well a microchip performs its job. For example, while SMD may fit better in compact devices, its fragile connections might struggle in high-vibration environments, like in cars. On the flip side, while DIP is more durable, it can't match the density and efficiency of newer packaging methods.

Choosing the right packaging is a lot like a chef picking ingredients for a dish. Each part needs to work well with the others to create the best outcome. The choice of packaging can control how a microchip handles environmental stress, how well it communicates with other components, and how efficiently it deals with power and heat. The stakes are high; picking the wrong packaging can lead to serious failures, costly recalls, and damage to a brand's reputation.

As technology moves forward and the push for smaller, faster, and more efficient devices grows, chip packaging is constantly changing. Engineers and designers are always on the hunt for new materials and techniques to improve packaging performance. For instance, advancements in polymer materials have created better thermal management strategies, helping microchips stay cool even under heavy use. Also, the rise of 3D packaging techniques allows chips to be stacked vertically, saving space and potentially enhancing performance due to shorter distances between connections.

Visual aids are incredibly helpful for grasping these concepts. Diagrams and illustrations that show different packaging types can help clarify the complexities involved. A well-designed image can illustrate how a BGA's solder balls connect to a PCB or how a COB setup looks in a compact wearable device. This visual representation is key to understanding the details of each method and appreciating the engineering choices behind them.

The world of chip packaging is anything but boring. It's a lively field that requires a solid understanding of materials, design principles, and the unique needs of various applications. As microchips become more and more important in our everyday lives, we can't overlook the significance of their packaging. It's a critical final step in the manufacturing process, ensuring microchips perform reliably across countless devices— from the smartphones we carry to the advanced computers powering artificial intelligence. Grasping the intricacies of chip packaging deepens our understanding of microchip technology, allowing us to appreciate how these devices work and the thoughtful design that goes into them. As technology keeps evolving, so will the methods and materials used in chip packaging, promising an exciting future for innovation and functionality in the world of microelectronics.

Mounting and Bonding

When we dive into the world of electronics, mounting and bonding microchips onto circuit boards is a lot like piecing together the final parts of a puzzle. Each microchip, much like a puzzle piece, needs to fit just right in its assigned spot on the board. This perfect fit is crucial for the final product—whether it's a smartphone, a tablet, or any other gadget—to be functional and dependable. It's not just about sticking components together; it's about building strong connections that can withstand the wear and tear of everyday use. This detailed process relies on two main techniques: soldering and adhesive bonding.

Soldering has been the go-to method for ages in the mounting process. Picture melting metal to create a solid connection— that's the heart of soldering. This technique involves using a filler metal, usually a mix of tin and lead, that melts at a lower temperature. Once it cools down, it hardens into a strong electrical link. There are two main techniques here: wave soldering and reflow soldering. Each comes with its own perks and challenges.

Wave soldering is a bit like a thrill ride for circuit boards. In this technique, a conveyor belt carries printed circuit boards (PCBs) over a wave of molten solder. As the board glides over this wave, the solder fills the holes and coats the component pins. This method is particularly good for through-hole components, which are often larger and need a sturdy connection to handle mechanical stress. But, like any ride, it has its bumps along the way. Sometimes, wave soldering can lead to solder bridging, where extra solder accidentally connects two or more points, risking short circuits.

On the other hand, reflow soldering is tailored for surface-mount technology (SMT) components. In this method, solder paste—a mixture of tiny solder balls and flux—is spread onto the PCB. After the components are positioned on the paste, everything goes into a reflow oven. The heat from the oven melts the solder, creating connections as it cools down. This technique allows for higher precision and is great for densely packed boards. However, reflow soldering isn't without its challenges. If the temperature isn't carefully managed, sensitive components can warp due to thermal stress, leading to problems later on.

While soldering is still widely used, adhesive bonding has become a strong alternative. This method uses special adhesives to securely attach microchips to their boards. Think of it like using glue instead of nails; the connection is strong, but it also brings benefits that soldering doesn't offer. Adhesive bonding provides flexibility, which is especially helpful in situations where thermal expansion and contraction could stress the connections. Plus, it can work with a wider variety of materials, which is crucial for innovative designs that use ceramics, plastics, or other non-metallic substrates.

Adhesive bonding comes in various forms, including epoxy, silicone, and polyurethane-based adhesives. Each of these materials has its own special traits that cater to different needs. For example, epoxy adhesives are known for their excellent thermal and chemical resistance, making them perfect for challenging environments. In contrast, silicone adhesives are incredibly flexible and can handle significant temperature changes—ideal for applications involving movement. However, adhesive bonding has its downsides, too. The bond might not hold up as well as a solder joint under extreme mechanical stress, and the curing process can make manufacturing timelines more complicated.

No matter which method is chosen, it's crucial to understand how important quality control is in the mounting and bonding process. Just like an architect wouldn't let a building go without thorough inspection, the electronics industry needs strict checks to ensure connection integrity. Even tiny defects can cause major failures in electronic devices, such as a complete system shutdown or erratic behavior. A problem in soldering could lead to a cold solder joint—where the solder doesn't fully stick to the microchip or PCB—while issues with adhesive bonding could result in delamination or weak connections that fail over time.

To make it easier to understand, think of mounting and bonding microchips like building a skyscraper. The foundation has to be solid, the beams need to fit perfectly, and every connection must be secure. If even one beam is misaligned or the foundation is weak, the whole structure could be at risk. Similarly, if a microchip isn't mounted or bonded correctly, it could fail, leading to costly repairs and damaging the manufacturer's reputation.

Furthermore, as electronics get smaller and the demand for miniaturization increases, mounting and bonding techniques must adapt to meet these challenges. Microelectromechanical systems (MEMS) and nanoelectronics are pushing the need for even more precise and reliable connections. The drive to create smaller and more efficient devices is changing the way engineers think about these processes, leading to new innovations that aim to improve durability while saving space.

Another important aspect to consider is thermal management in the mounting and bonding processes. Microchips produce heat, and how that heat is managed can greatly affect their performance. Poorly mounted chips can create hot spots, leading to thermal runaway, where heat builds up uncontrollably, potentially causing failures or, in extreme cases, fires. Engineers must think about heat sinks, thermal pads, and other heat management strategies when designing the mounting and bonding processes.

Visualizing these ideas can really help. Diagrams or photographs can clarify the different techniques used in mounting and bonding. A well-crafted image can effectively show how solder flows during wave soldering or how adhesive spreads under a microchip, helping to highlight the specifics of each method. Being able to see the process helps deepen our understanding of how microchips connect to circuit boards and what these connections mean for the final product.

In short, mounting and bonding microchips to circuit boards is a crucial part of microchip manufacturing. It requires a careful blend of engineering precision, material science, and rigorous quality control. Whether through soldering, with its long-standing trustworthiness, or adhesive bonding, with its flexibility and innovative applications, the bond between microchips and circuit boards is where functionality begins. As technology evolves, these processes must change, ensuring that our electronic devices stay reliable and efficient in a fast-paced world. So, the next time you pick up your smartphone or power on your laptop, take a moment to appreciate the hidden work that goes into making those devices function smoothly—where each microchip is securely mounted and bonded, creating the foundation of the technology we depend on every day.

Final Integration

In the world of electronics, putting microchips into larger systems is like mixing the final ingredients in a delicious recipe. Each part must not only add to the overall flavor but also work well together to create a smooth experience. This last stage of integration is super important because it involves several steps that ensure the microchips perform their best in the electronic world.

At the core of this integration are three key elements: power distribution, signal integrity, and thermal management. While these might sound like complicated words, they're really the heartbeat of any electronic device, making sure the microchips run reliably, efficiently, and safely. Think about it:

without proper power distribution, even the most advanced microchip would be as useful as a paperweight.

Power distribution might seem boring, but it's actually the foundation of any electronic system. Microchips need a steady flow of electricity to work, and how that power is managed can make a big difference. Picture a finely tuned orchestra: if one musician plays too loudly, it can drown out everyone else, turning harmony into chaos. In the same way, microchips need just the right amount of power—not too little, or they might not work, and not too much, or they risk overheating or damaging delicate parts.

The process starts with designing the power distribution network, which can be pretty tricky. Engineers have to think about things like voltage needs, current load, and how the circuit board is laid out. Smart techniques, like power gating and dynamic voltage scaling, help make this distribution more efficient. For instance, power gating allows parts of a chip to be turned off when they're not needed, which cuts down on energy use significantly.

On the other hand, dynamic voltage scaling adjusts the voltage sent to the microchip based on what it's doing. If a chip is just sitting idle, it might need only a tiny bit of power compared to when it's working hard on complex tasks. By managing power distribution in this smart way, engineers can boost performance and energy efficiency, which means longer battery life for portable gadgets—something we all care about in today's mobile-focused lifestyle.

As we dig deeper into the integration process, we come to the important topic of signal integrity. In a world where communication is quick and constant, it's crucial for microchips to send and receive signals clearly. Think of signal integrity like having a clear conversation in a noisy room. If there's too much background noise, you can miss important points, which can lead to misunderstandings or even complete breakdowns in communication.

Achieving good signal integrity requires careful design and layout of the electronic circuits. Engineers need to consider the paths signals will take, making sure they are as direct and clear as possible. This involves looking at things like trace width, impedance matching, and the materials used for the circuit board. The goal is to reduce reflections, crosstalk, and electromagnetic interference—those annoying little issues that can disrupt electronic communication.

Proper grounding and shielding are also key to maintaining signal integrity. Grounding gives signals a reference point, which helps stabilize them, while shielding protects sensitive components from outside noise. Designing a circuit layout that maximizes signal integrity is part science, part art. The best designs are not just functional but also beautifully simple, showcasing a deep understanding of the principles at play.

Another essential part of final integration is managing heat. Microchips work hard, and the heat they generate can be a double-edged sword. While heat is a natural byproduct of their operation, too much of it can cause performance issues, system instability, or even total failure. So, engineers need to find effective ways to dissipate heat, allowing microchips to perform optimally without overheating.

There are many strategies for thermal management. Heat sinks, often made of materials like aluminum or copper, are commonly used to pull heat away from components. These metal structures increase the surface area available for losing heat, helping to transfer it to the surrounding air more effectively. Sometimes, thermal pads or thermal interface materials (TIMs) are added to improve the connection between the chip and the heat sink, allowing for better heat transfer.

In demanding situations, engineers might use active cooling methods like fans or liquid cooling systems. These systems help circulate air or coolant around the microchips to keep temperatures within safe limits. While these solutions can be more complex and costly, they can also greatly extend the lifespan and reliability of high-performance systems.

Engineers also have to think about how heat interacts across the entire system, not just with individual parts. The way microchips and other heat-producing elements are placed is crucial to making sure heat is spread evenly and doesn't create hot spots. This means taking a big-picture approach, viewing the entire assembly as a living ecosystem rather than just a bunch of separate parts.

With power distribution, signal integrity, and thermal management all working together in the integration process, quality assurance becomes a crucial step in this final stage. Testing microchips and their systems isn't just a box to check; it's a vital step that can prevent major issues down the road.

Thorough testing processes are essential to make sure each microchip meets performance standards before it reaches the market. This could mean stress-testing under extreme conditions or simulating different operational scenarios to see how the chip behaves. Engineers carefully examine everything, from power use and heat generation to signal clarity and overall system stability.

The real-world importance of rigorous testing can't be overstated. Imagine if a chip fails in a consumer device, leading to a frustrating experience for the user. Maybe the device crashes right when you need it most—like navigating through a busy street or streaming your favorite show. The consequences of such failures can erode consumer trust and lead to significant financial losses for manufacturers.

Take, for example, a recent incident in the automotive industry where a microchip failed, causing a safety system to malfunction. The fallout was severe, leading to recalls and a lot of negative media attention. It serves as a strong reminder of what's at stake when it comes to microchip integration. Each chip that rolls off the production line has the potential to impact lives.

To illustrate this further, consider the healthcare field, where microchips are essential in devices like pacemakers and insulin pumps. If a chip fails in these critical applications, the results can be life-threatening. This is why the testing and quality assurance phase is treated with utmost seriousness; it can literally be a matter of life and death.

The integration of microchips into electronic systems is a detailed and multifaceted process that demands careful planning and execution. It's a coordinated effort that includes power distribution, signal integrity, thermal management, and thorough testing, all working together to ensure microchips operate effectively in their larger electronic context.

As technology keeps advancing, the importance of final integration will only increase. Our world relies more and more on microchips, from smartphones to smart homes and even self-driving cars. Understanding how these systems work helps us appreciate the careful work that goes into creating the technology we use every day.

So, next time you turn on your device or use some technology, take a moment to think about the incredible journey each microchip has taken—through power distribution, signal integrity, thermal management, and testing—before it became a reliable part of your life. The hard work of engineers and designers is what turns ideas into the seamless technology we often take for granted.

Ethan Maxwell

Chapter 9: The Business of Chip Making

The Semiconductor Industry

The world of microchips is truly captivating, where brilliant engineering meets sharp business skills. The semiconductor industry, often seen as the foundation of modern technology, plays a vital role in our everyday lives. From the smartphones we hold onto like lifelines to the advanced cars that zoom down our streets, all rely on a multitude of chips. This industry not only drives innovation but also shapes economies and global relationships, affecting everything from what we buy to how countries interact with each other.

At its heart, the semiconductor industry is a vast network of companies that create and produce semiconductor devices, mainly microchips. Over the past few decades, this global market has surged, now reaching a stunning value in the hundreds of billions of dollars. This rapid growth is fueled by an unending appetite for electronics, driven by shifting consumer preferences and the fast pace of technological progress. Reports indicate that the semiconductor market was valued at around $440 billion in 2020, and it's expected to soar past $1 trillion by the end of the decade, highlighting its crucial role in the global economy.

The industry is filled with key players that compete and collaborate in exciting ways. Major companies like Intel, Samsung, and Taiwan Semiconductor Manufacturing Company (TSMC) are leading the charge, each playing unique yet interconnected roles in the semiconductor world. Intel, often hailed as the leader in modern computing, specializes in designing and making microprocessors, which act as the brains of our computers. For years, Intel has maintained a strong grip on the market, always pushing the limits of performance and energy efficiency.

Next, we have Samsung, a giant not just in semiconductors but across the wider electronics industry. While it produces a broad range of products, its semiconductor division stands out for its memory chips, which are essential in everything from personal gadgets to massive data centers. Samsung's size and commitment to innovation help it stay ahead, often engaging in tough competition with other memory chip makers like Micron and SK Hynix.

Meanwhile, TSMC has become a powerhouse in semiconductor manufacturing, especially known for its foundry services. Unlike Intel and Samsung, which both design and manufacture their chips, TSMC focuses solely on making chips for other companies. This unique business model has made TSMC a crucial partner for many fabless semiconductor firms, such as Qualcomm, AMD, and Nvidia. The industry thrives on collaboration, with different companies specializing in various parts of chip development and production, creating a complex ecosystem that is both reliant on each other and fiercely competitive.

The economic importance of the semiconductor sector is truly remarkable. Beyond its direct contributions to GDP and job creation, it acts as a key support for many other industries, including automotive, telecommunications, consumer electronics, and even healthcare. The industry doesn't just make chips; it includes a wide array of activities like research and development (R&D), marketing, and supply chain logistics—all vital for successfully launching and adopting new technologies. As microchips continue to shrink, become more powerful, and find their way into every aspect of our lives, the need for innovation in this field will only rise.

Investment in the semiconductor industry reflects its significance. Venture capitalists and private equity firms are eager to back startups that promise breakthroughs in semiconductor technology, whether through new materials, advanced manufacturing techniques, or creative applications. Governments are also stepping up, realizing that strong semiconductor capabilities are crucial for national security and technological independence. As a result, initiatives are popping up to boost domestic semiconductor production, seen as a way to reduce reliance on foreign supply chains, especially after the recent disruptions in global supply chains.

Geopolitical issues also heavily influence the landscape of the semiconductor industry. The competition between the United States and China has raised the stakes in this sector. China has invested significantly in building its semiconductor infrastructure, aiming for self-reliance in chip production. This ambition has led the U.S. to tighten restrictions on technology exports, especially regarding advanced semiconductor technologies. These trade tensions have rippled through the industry, affecting supply chains and causing companies to rethink their manufacturing strategies.

We can't ignore the pressing challenges facing the semiconductor industry. The global

COVID-19 pandemic exposed vulnerabilities within supply chains, resulting in shortages that affected everything from consumer electronics to automotive production. Manufacturers struggled to keep up with booming demand while dealing with logistical challenges, revealing just how interconnected and fragile the industry can be. This situation has sparked renewed calls for investment in domestic semiconductor production to ensure we are better prepared for future disruptions.

Sustainability has also risen to the forefront of industry concerns. Manufacturing semiconductors is resource-intensive, using large amounts of water and energy. As awareness of climate change increases, semiconductor companies are feeling the heat to adopt more eco-friendly practices and minimize their environmental footprint. This includes investing in renewable energy, improving water conservation, and finding ways to make manufacturing processes more efficient. Moving toward sustainable practices isn't just a trend; it's becoming a necessity in a world that demands accountability from industries everywhere.

To wrap it all up, the semiconductor industry is a vibrant and complex network of innovation, competition, and cooperation. It's a sector that not only powers our devices but also fuels economies and shapes global relations. As the need for smarter and more efficient technology grows, the industry will keep evolving, pushing the limits of what's possible while tackling challenges around sustainability, supply chain resilience, and geopolitical issues. The journey of microchips—from their initial conception to everyday use—not only showcases the wonders of engineering but also underscores the significant impact semiconductors have on our connected world. The future of technology relies on this industry, and getting to know its intricacies is vital for anyone keen on understanding the changing landscape of modern life.

Research and Development

In the fast-paced world of microchip technology, research and development (R&D) is truly the lifeblood of innovation. Companies of all sizes invest heavily in R&D, aiming not just to keep up with their rivals but to leap ahead with groundbreaking advancements. The stakes are incredibly high— fortunes are at risk based on the ability to create chips that are not only faster and more efficient but also more powerful. This relentless drive for progress turns early ideas into state-of-the-art products that reshape the tech landscape.

The process of R&D in chip manufacturing is a complicated journey that unfolds through several stages. It all starts with foundational research, where scientists and engineers challenge the limits of what's possible. This stage often involves experimenting with new materials, designs, and techniques. A prime example is the exploration of graphene, a remarkable material with exceptional conductivity and flexibility, as a potential replacement for traditional silicon in semiconductors. Researchers are excited by graphene's possibilities, imagining a future where it could create chips that are quicker and more energy-efficient.

Once the foundational research shows promise, the next step is prototyping. This phase breathes life into the ideas, transforming initial designs into physical prototypes. Engineers carefully create the first versions of the chips, ready for testing and improvement. This back-and-forth process is akin to sculpting, requiring patience and precision as various prototypes are produced, tested, and tweaked based on performance feedback. The objective is to pinpoint any flaws and fine-tune the design, ensuring the final product is solid and effective.

Testing is the final piece of this crucial R&D phase. This is where ideas are put to the test in real-world situations. Performance metrics like power usage, speed, and heat management are closely examined. Teamwork is essential here, as design engineers collaborate with test engineers to analyze data, solve problems, and refine designs. It's a dynamic partnership that turns raw materials into ready-to-market products, illustrating the delicate balance between creativity and scientific discipline in R&D.

To highlight how R&D impacts chip technology, consider the shift from 10nm to 7nm and then to 5nm manufacturing processes. Each new process brings about a substantial improvement in efficiency and performance. These advancements don't just mean smaller transistors; they also reflect major engineering breakthroughs. For instance, the use of extreme ultraviolet (EUV) lithography has revolutionized chip manufacturing, allowing for the production of chips with unmatched precision and density. This innovation showcases the power of R&D, enabling companies to fit more transistors in a small chip area, boosting performance while keeping power use low.

Creating chips that are faster, smaller, and more capable isn't just an end goal; it carries significant implications across many industries. We see the effects of these advancements everywhere—from smartphones with incredibly speedy processors to the servers that drive cloud computing, supporting everything from social media to artificial intelligence. In this light, R&D becomes a key player in economic growth, as companies that lead in innovation generate jobs, attract investment, and strengthen entire supply chains.

Collaboration between universities and industry also plays a crucial role in advancing R&D in semiconductors. Universities are breeding grounds for fresh ideas, filled with brilliant minds exploring theoretical concepts that can eventually be put to practical use. Partnerships between academic institutions and tech firms create a mutually beneficial dynamic, where academic research supports commercial projects, while industry challenges inspire new academic pursuits. Programs that promote this collaboration often lead to groundbreaking discoveries, creating a steady flow of talent and ideas that drive the industry forward.

One standout example of this successful collaboration is the partnership between MIT and various semiconductor companies. Their joint research efforts have led to significant progress in areas like quantum computing and neuromorphic chips—devices designed to mimic how the human brain's neural networks work. These partnerships highlight how sharing resources and insights can lead to innovative breakthroughs that benefit both academia and the industry, resulting in a more skilled workforce and an ever-evolving world of chip technology.

The importance of intellectual property (IP) in R&D cannot be underestimated. As companies pour resources into research and innovation, protecting their inventions through patents is a top priority. Patents act as a shield, safeguarding the hard-won innovations that could give them a competitive edge. In an industry where ideas and technology can be easily copied, having a strong IP portfolio is vital. This protection not only helps companies secure their investments but also attracts partnerships and funding, ensuring they can enjoy the financial rewards of their innovations.

A clear example of the significance of IP in semiconductor R&D is the ongoing rivalry between Nvidia and AMD. Nvidia has made great strides in developing graphics processing units (GPUs) and artificial intelligence (AI) technologies. Their careful approach to R&D has resulted in numerous patented innovations that boost performance in gaming, data science, and machine learning. Meanwhile, AMD has been revitalizing its R&D efforts to catch up with Nvidia. This competition drives both companies to innovate more rapidly, ultimately benefiting consumers and businesses alike.

Yet, the path of R&D in the semiconductor industry is filled with challenges. The costs associated with research and development can be astronomical. Building an advanced semiconductor fabrication facility can require billions in investment, along with ongoing expenses for research and talent acquisition. Plus, moving from a concept to actual production can take years, with no guarantees of success. This reality creates a high-stakes environment where companies must constantly reassess their strategies and adapt to the fast-changing tech landscape.

Additionally, the rapid pace of technological change brings its own set of challenges for R&D teams. With new innovations popping up at lightning speed, companies need to remain flexible and responsive. This requires significant investment in talent, as organizations strive to attract the brightest minds who can envision and implement groundbreaking solutions. The semiconductor industry thus becomes a hub for engineers, researchers, and scientists, all eager to be part of the next technological breakthrough.

Investing in R&D isn't just for private companies. Governments, recognizing the vital role of semiconductor technology for national security and economic stability, have begun to invest heavily in research initiatives. This trend has been particularly notable in the United States, where federal funding is being allocated to support semiconductor R&D. These initiatives aim to boost domestic capabilities and lessen reliance on foreign supply chains, especially given recent global disruptions.

The need to strengthen domestic semiconductor capabilities has led to a renewed focus on STEM (science, technology, engineering, and mathematics) education. As the industry expands, so does the demand for a skilled workforce that can drive innovation. Educational institutions are adjusting their curricula to align with industry needs, ensuring future engineers and scientists are prepared to tackle the challenges of microchip development.

Moreover, the global semiconductor industry is navigating a complex landscape marked by geopolitical tensions and environmental considerations. The rush to innovate is often balanced against the need for sustainability, as semiconductor manufacturing can be resource-heavy. Companies are under pressure to adopt eco-friendly practices, which may involve investing in energy-saving technologies, improving waste management, and embracing circular economy principles. This shift toward sustainability not only aids the planet but also enhances a company's reputation and attracts environmentally aware consumers.

The intricate relationship between research, development, and sustainability is becoming a defining feature of successful semiconductor strategies. As companies look ahead, they must balance the urge to innovate with the need for responsible manufacturing. This dual focus can lead to exciting advancements, like developing chips that are not only more efficient and consume less power but also utilize sustainable materials.

In the end, R&D in the chip-making industry is a rich and complex endeavor that captures the spirit of innovation in our modern world. It encompasses everything from fundamental research and prototyping to protecting intellectual property and fostering collaboration between academia and industry. The investments made in R&D not only drive technological progress but also have significant impacts on global economies, job creation, and sustainable practices.

The quest for excellence in semiconductor technology is a relentless journey, filled with creativity, teamwork, and a steadfast commitment to pushing the limits of what's possible. As the industry continues to evolve, the stories of innovation born from R&D will shape the devices we use, the industries we support, and the future we imagine. In a world where microchips are central to nearly every aspect of our lives, grasping the details of research and development is key to appreciating the incredible technologies that propel our society forward. Each achievement is a step toward a future where technology not only meets our needs but also sparks our creativity and challenges us to dream even bigger.

Challenges and Solutions

The semiconductor industry plays a vital role in driving modern technology, but it also faces several challenges that could impact its stability and growth. Recently, these challenges have become more pronounced, exposing weaknesses that can disrupt many areas of our economy. The COVID-19 pandemic acted like a magnifying glass, highlighting just how fragile global supply chains really are. As lockdowns took effect and factories closed, the semiconductor industry faced major supply chain disruptions, leading to consequences that rippled out beyond just the tech sector.

One clear example of these disruptions can be found in the automotive industry. Once thought of as a separate field, the automotive sector is now deeply tied to the semiconductor industry. Today's vehicles rely on numerous chips for everything from engine performance to entertainment systems. When semiconductor production slowed down, car manufacturers suddenly found themselves in a tight spot, facing a severe shortage of essential components. Production lines ground to a halt, leaving many unfinished cars sitting unused in factories. The impact was widespread—orders were canceled, prices soared, and the availability of new cars dropped significantly. The fallout from semiconductor shortages affected not just vehicles, but also a wide array of consumer goods, highlighting how interconnected our modern economy has become.

As the industry struggles with these supply chain issues, it is also facing increased scrutiny over its environmental impact. Semiconductor manufacturing is known for being energy-intensive and producing a lot of waste, raising serious concerns about sustainability. The industry must face the reality that its operations contribute to carbon emissions and electronic waste, both of which are urgent global challenges. This recognition has sparked conversations about how to create a more sustainable semiconductor landscape.

In chip manufacturing, the energy used during production is immense. Estimates suggest that the semiconductor manufacturing process can consume as much energy as a small city. As more businesses embrace digital technology, the demand for energy continues to rise. This puts pressure on semiconductor companies to shift towards cleaner energy sources and adopt practices that reduce their carbon footprint. Some companies are investing in renewable energy, while others are looking into more energy-efficient manufacturing methods. With the rollout of 5G and the Internet of Things (IoT), the need for semiconductors has only grown, emphasizing the importance of balancing industry growth with responsible manufacturing.

To tackle these challenges, industry leaders are finding creative ways to improve efficiency and build resilience. One key strategy gaining traction is diversifying supply chains. Companies are increasingly aware of the risks that come with relying too heavily on a single region or supplier for their semiconductor needs. The pandemic highlighted the dangers of such dependencies, prompting many to seek alternative sources for their chips. This shift not only reduces risk but also encourages competition, potentially leading to better pricing and innovation.

Artificial intelligence (AI) and machine learning are also making a significant impact in the semiconductor industry. By using these advanced technologies, companies can enhance their ability to predict demand and manage inventory more effectively. This proactive approach helps to minimize waste and streamline production processes. Being able to anticipate market changes and adjust accordingly is a crucial step toward securing a bright future for the industry.

Governments, too, are stepping up to address the challenges facing the semiconductor sector. Many countries recognize how important semiconductors are for national security and economic stability, leading them to invest in domestic manufacturing capabilities. This effort aims to decrease reliance on foreign suppliers and strengthen local supply chains. For instance, in the United States, lawmakers are pushing for increased funding for semiconductor research and development, along with incentives for companies to grow their manufacturing operations at home.

These government-supported initiatives can help create a more robust semiconductor ecosystem. By encouraging collaboration between public and private sectors, the industry will be better prepared for future challenges. Such partnerships could lead to policies that support innovation while ensuring that environmental concerns are prioritized. In this way, the industry can evolve alongside the growing demand for sustainable practices.

The urgent need for sustainability is driving semiconductor companies to adopt greener practices. Some manufacturers are introducing recycling programs for old chips, which helps to reduce electronic waste. These efforts aim to recover valuable materials from discarded chips, creating a circular economy where resources are reused rather than thrown away. Additionally, advancements in materials science are paving the way for more sustainable manufacturing processes. Companies are researching alternatives to traditional materials, including biodegradable substances or materials that require less energy to produce.

Beyond these innovative practices, many semiconductor firms are also working to improve transparency in their supply chains. By implementing stricter sourcing standards and monitoring suppliers, they can lessen the environmental impact of their operations. This commitment to sustainability can resonate with consumers who increasingly prefer brands that prioritize eco-friendly practices. As awareness of climate change grows, companies that weave sustainability into their business models may find themselves in a stronger position to succeed in a competitive market.

However, the semiconductor industry is not only challenged by supply chain issues or environmental concerns; it also faces market dynamics. The rapid pace of technological advancements means companies must constantly innovate or risk falling behind. As consumer expectations rise, driven by a demand for faster and more powerful devices, companies need to stay nimble. The race to develop cutting-edge technology creates fierce competition, and failing to keep up can lead to significant setbacks.

To counter these risks, companies are increasingly looking to collaboration. Forming strategic partnerships between semiconductor manufacturers, tech firms, and research institutions can boost innovation and speed up the development of new technologies. By sharing resources and expertise, these collaborations can tackle industry-wide challenges more effectively. For example, partnerships between semiconductor companies and universities have already proven beneficial in driving research that can lead to breakthroughs in chip technology.

The semiconductor industry is also seeing a surge in investment from venture capital firms. These investors recognize the potential for growth in the sector and are eager to support innovative startups that can help shape its future. The influx of funding can empower these emerging companies to develop groundbreaking technologies and create products that address current issues. By backing the next wave of innovators, venture capitalists can play a crucial role in steering the semiconductor landscape toward new horizons.

As the industry moves forward, focusing on workforce development will become increasingly important. With the demand for skilled talent in semiconductor manufacturing expected to rise sharply, it's essential to build a strong and capable workforce. Companies and educational institutions need to work together to create training programs that equip workers for the challenges within the semiconductor sector. By investing in education and skill development, the industry can cultivate a pool of talented professionals ready to drive innovation and tackle emerging challenges.

The intersection of these challenges and solutions paints a complex yet dynamic picture of the semiconductor industry. As companies navigate supply chain issues, sustainability concerns, and market pressures, they are discovering new pathways for collaboration and innovation. The future of the semiconductor industry depends on its ability to adapt and evolve in response to these obstacles. By welcoming innovative solutions, fostering collaboration, and prioritizing sustainability, the semiconductor industry can prepare itself for growth and success in the years to come.

In light of these many challenges, it's important to recognize the creativity and determination of the companies and individuals working to overcome them. The semiconductor industry stands at a pivotal moment, where today's decisions will shape tomorrow's technological landscape. As it confronts these pressing issues, there's a real opportunity for it to emerge stronger, more efficient, and more sustainable, setting the stage for a future where microchips continue to enhance our lives in remarkable ways. The road ahead may be tough, but with innovation and collaboration guiding the way, the semiconductor industry is ready to tackle the challenges that lie ahead.

Ethan Maxwell

Chapter 10: The Future of Microchips

Emerging Technologies

The world of microchips is constantly changing, and as we enter a new era of technology, the innovations on the horizon are set to transform how we understand computation and intelligence. Two of the most intriguing advancements we're seeing are quantum computing and neuromorphic chips. These technologies are not just small steps forward; they represent significant shifts in how we tackle problems and interact with the world around us.

Let's start with quantum computing. This technology challenges everything we thought we knew about traditional computers. Regular computers, which are built on silicon and binary logic, process information in a straightforward way, using bits that are either 0s or 1s. This binary system has been the backbone of computing, powering everything from simple calculators to supercomputers. But quantum computers flip this idea on its head. Instead of bits, they use qubits, which can exist in multiple states at once thanks to the strange rules of quantum mechanics. This unique ability, known as superposition, lets quantum computers handle massive amounts of data at incredible speeds, dramatically boosting their computational power.

Think about the potential here. What if cryptography—a key part of keeping our online communications secure—could be completely transformed overnight? With quantum computing, problems that would take today's fastest supercomputers thousands of years to solve might be figured out in just a few seconds. This isn't just a dream; companies like IBM and Google are racing to create quantum processors that can tackle ever more complex challenges. We're on the brink of what could be a quantum revolution. Fields like materials science could be completely changed as well. Researchers could simulate molecular interactions with unmatched precision, leading to the creation of new materials that could revolutionize everything from aerospace to healthcare.

However, it's important to keep in mind that while the prospects of quantum computing are exciting, there are still hurdles to overcome. The current generation of quantum computers is still in its early stages and faces challenges like qubit stability and higher error rates compared to classical computers. The race for quantum supremacy— where a quantum computer does a job better than the best classical computers—is ongoing. Until we reach this point, we won't fully realize the potential of quantum technology.

Now, let's shift our focus from quantum mechanics to neuromorphic computing, which brings us to a different yet equally captivating idea. Neuromorphic chips are designed to imitate the way our brains work. They use a network of artificial neurons and synapses to process information in a way that differs fundamentally from traditional silicon chips. Rather than following a linear approach, neuromorphic systems operate using parallel processing. This allows them to tackle complex tasks like recognizing patterns and analyzing sensory data with impressive efficiency.

The potential of neuromorphic technology is enormous, especially in the field of artificial intelligence. Current AI systems often rely on deep learning algorithms that need huge amounts of data and extensive training. In contrast, neuromorphic chips can learn and adapt in ways that are reminiscent of how humans think, enabling machines to recognize patterns, make decisions, and even predict outcomes with minimal input. This could pave the way for more intuitive AI systems that can understand and respond to human emotions, changing how we interact with technology every day.

Consider how neuromorphic chips could reshape healthcare. These advanced systems might be able to process medical imaging data almost instantly, spotting issues that human doctors could overlook. When paired with the power of quantum computing, we could enter a future where personalized medicine isn't just a concept but a reality— imagine treatment plans tailored to each person in real time, taking into account their genetic makeup, lifestyle, and environment.

As we explore these two groundbreaking technologies, we also need to think about the ethical questions they raise and how they will affect the future of work. What will happen to traditional job roles as machines become capable of thinking and learning like humans? Will society be ready for a world where AI outperforms us in tasks we once believed required a human touch? The answers are complicated and involve not just technology but also our values and economic systems.

Beyond job markets, there are broader ethical concerns we must address. As we create smarter machines, we need to consider issues of control, accountability, and the moral aspects of artificial intelligence. It will be crucial to ensure transparency and fairness in the algorithms that drive these systems to avoid the biases and discrimination that have already surfaced in some current AI applications.

In looking ahead at the world of microchip technology, we're standing at the edge of a revolution where quantum computing and neuromorphic chips represent exciting possibilities. These technologies challenge traditional ideas about computation and open up new opportunities to enhance our lives in ways we're just starting to grasp. But with this potential comes the responsibility to approach these innovations thoughtfully and ethically. As we move forward, we must remain aware of the societal impacts that come with these advances. The future of microchips isn't just about faster processors or more powerful computations; it's about rethinking our relationship with technology itself.

Innovations in Fabrication

As the demand for more powerful and efficient microchips keeps growing, the limits of traditional silicon-based technologies are becoming clearer. The ongoing quest for smaller, faster, and more energy-efficient chips has pushed researchers and engineers to look into advanced fabrication techniques. These new methods aren't just minor tweaks; they could completely change the world of semiconductor technology.

One of the most exciting developments is the idea of stacking chips in three dimensions. Picture a standard two-dimensional circuit board crammed with components. Now, imagine that same setup, but instead of spreading everything out flat, the components are stacked on top of each other. This three-dimensional stacking, often called 3D chip architecture, allows for a significant boost in functionality without making devices any bigger.

The perks of 3D stacking go far beyond just saving space. With components packed closer together, data can zip around faster, cutting down on delays and boosting overall performance. Think about it like this: if you're trying to share a secret across a large room, you might have to shout. But if you lean in closer, you can share your thoughts much more quickly and clearly. In the same way, 3D stacked chips can communicate with each other in a fraction of the time, leading to faster and better performance.

Building these stacked chips is no small feat. It requires careful assembly using advanced techniques that involve tiny manipulations and precise alignments. It's like constructing a delicate tower where each level has to fit together perfectly to ensure stability and functionality. Engineers use different bonding methods to hold the layers together and incorporate advanced thermal management systems to keep heat in check.

This careful craftsmanship results in devices that are not only powerful but also reliable in tough conditions.

Yet, while 3D stacking is fascinating, it's just one part of a bigger picture. Another groundbreaking technique is extreme ultraviolet (EUV) lithography. This advanced method allows manufacturers to etch fine circuits on chips with extraordinary precision. Traditional photolithography techniques have hit a wall, struggling to create the tiny features needed for today's chips. EUV lithography directly tackles this issue by using light with a very short wavelength, which allows for smaller and more intricate circuit patterns.

To understand the importance of EUV lithography, let's think about photography. Imagine taking a picture of a landscape with a low-resolution camera. The details would look fuzzy and unclear. Now picture upgrading to a high-resolution camera that captures even the smallest details, creating vibrant and crystal-clear images. EUV lithography works in much the same way, using advanced optics and light sources to produce sharp, detailed patterns on silicon wafers.

The EUV process involves several steps. First, a photosensitive material is applied to the wafer. Then, light from the EUV source is projected through special optics onto the wafer, exposing specific areas. After exposure, a development process uncovers the desired patterns for the circuits. The end result? A chip with tightly packed, intricate features that enables more powerful and energy-efficient devices.

The impact of EUV lithography is massive. With each new chip generation, as transistors shrink and complex features are added, the capabilities of our electronic devices expand. Smartphones get faster and more efficient, computers tackle more demanding tasks, and innovations like the Internet of Things (IoT) continue to grow. But while we explore these advances, we also need to keep an eye on the materials used to create these intricate circuits.

Silicon has been the backbone of semiconductor technology for a long time, but it comes with its own set of challenges. New materials like graphene and carbon nanotubes are stepping in, showing the potential to transform chip performance. Graphene, a single layer of carbon atoms arranged in a two-dimensional formation, is renowned for its excellent electrical conductivity and strength. This amazing material allows for faster electron movement, which could lead to chips that run faster and use less power.

Similarly, carbon nanotubes—tiny cylindrical structures made from graphene—display remarkable electrical properties. They can work effectively as transistors, making them a possible replacement for silicon in future chip designs. Plus, these materials have added benefits like flexibility and lightweight characteristics, making them perfect for wearable technology and flexible electronics.

The buzz around these new materials is exciting, but they also come with challenges. The manufacturing methods for integrating graphene and carbon nanotubes into existing semiconductor processes are still being improved. Researchers are hard at work finding scalable techniques that can produce high-quality materials while ensuring they fit in with current fabrication methods. This ongoing challenge highlights the ever-changing field of microchip innovation, where these new materials could shape the future of technology.

As we consider the future of chip fabrication, we can't overlook the environmental impact of these advancements. The semiconductor industry has faced criticism for its energy use and waste production. However, there's a growing awareness of the need for sustainable practices in manufacturing.

Innovations in fabrication techniques are increasingly being combined with eco-friendly practices aimed at reducing the industry's environmental footprint. For example, companies are adopting energy-efficient manufacturing processes that cut down on waste and lower greenhouse gas emissions. The move towards renewable energy sources in semiconductor manufacturing plants is gaining momentum, with organizations investing in solar, wind, and other sustainable energy options to power their operations.

Additionally, there's a strong focus on recycling materials in the production process. Key elements like rare earth metals, essential for microchip production, are being sourced from recycled materials instead of mined from the earth. This approach not only conserves natural resources but also reduces the environmental damage associated with mining.

The conversation about sustainability in semiconductor fabrication is becoming a key part of innovation. Industry leaders are beginning to understand that responsible manufacturing practices must go hand in hand with technological progress. Integrating environmentally friendly methods isn't just a passing trend; it's a vital step towards making sure the benefits of innovation don't come at the expense of our planet.

As we navigate the exciting world of chip fabrication innovations, it's clear that the future is full of opportunities. Breakthrough techniques like 3D stacking and EUV lithography offer a promising glimpse into a future where microchips become faster, smaller, and more energy-efficient. Exploring new materials like graphene and carbon nanotubes could lead to significant enhancements in performance, while sustainable practices ensure that these advancements are made responsibly.

Overall, these innovations in chip fabrication offer a chance to transform not only how we create technology but also how we interact with it. The journey of microchip evolution showcases human creativity—a relentless drive to improve that pushes the limits of what's possible. As we continue to innovate, we must stay mindful of our responsibilities to society and the environment, paving the way for a future where technology becomes a powerful ally for good. The story of innovation in chip fabrication is still unfolding, and there's a world of potential just waiting to be explored.

Conclusion

As we close the final chapter on our exploration of microchips, we stand at the threshold of an exciting future. The journey through the intricate world of silicon has revealed not just the complexity of these tiny marvels, but their profound impact on our lives and the boundless potential they hold.

From the meticulous design process to the precision of manufacturing, we've seen how microchips embody human ingenuity and relentless innovation. These silent workhorses of the digital age continue to evolve, promising advancements that will reshape industries, enhance our daily experiences, and tackle global challenges.

As you look around, notice how microchips have woven themselves into the fabric of your world. They're in your pocket, your home, your workplace – constantly working to make life easier, safer, and more connected. The next time you use your favorite gadget or benefit from a technological breakthrough, take a moment to appreciate the incredible journey from sand to silicon that made it possible.

The story of microchips is far from over. As we stand on the cusp of new frontiers in quantum computing, artificial intelligence, and beyond, the humble microchip will continue to be at the heart of these revolutions. What wonders will the next generation of chips bring? The answer lies in the imagination and determination of innovators yet to come – perhaps even you.

Ethan Maxwell

www.ingramcontent.com/pod-product-compliance
Lightning Source LLC
LaVergne TN
LVHW051334050326
832903LV00031B/3534